Walking from Ga⸱⸱⸱g and Wyresdale

Walking from Garstang and Wyresdale

Ian & Krysia Brodie

Carnegie Publishing

© Ian & Krysia Brodie, 2000

Published by Carnegie Publishing Ltd
Carnegie House, Chatsworth Road
Lancaster LA1 4SL
Tel: 01524-840111
Fax: 01524-840222
email: carnegie@provider.co.uk
web: www.carnegiepub.co.uk

First edition, 1986
Fourth edition, 2000

ISBN 1-85936-076-9

Typeset by Carnegie Publishing
Printed by The Cromwell Press, Wiltshire

Contents

Introduction

Welcome to the fourth edition of *Walking from Garstang*. The first edition appeared in 1986 and partially owed its origins to *Forty Rambles* by Bruce Clucas, the seventh and final edition of which Ian was priviliged to produce. The various editions of that book, which appeared from 1933, helped many Lancashire ramblers' explore their local countryside.

This edition of *Walking from Garstang* is much more extensively rewritten than its predecessors and we have been helped by living away from the area of the book and thereby being able to take a fresh look at the walks. There have been other matters that have encouraged this latest edition but we have still included the favourite routes from the earlier books. The changes include:

¤ the opening of the full 41-mile Wyre Way footpath by Wyre Borough Council. The first nine circular walks enable you to follow the full route of this walk downstream;

¤ the increasing use of public transport so that walks are more accessible to non car owners;

¤ changes to the rights of way network, too often occasioned by new demands for privacy from increasingly gentrified former farmsteads, and the availability of new permissive footpaths.

The area of the book is one of fine, contrasting landscapes, from moorland down to the coast, across undulating farmland and flat mosslands. Each landscape has a history to tell. The excellent work of Wyre Borough Council's Countryside Service and Lancashire County Council's Forest of Bowland Countryside teams have vastly improved the ease of use of the footpath network. They deserve recognition of their achievements.

All distances given are approximate and we have included at the end of each paragraph a rough estimate of the distance covered in the route description. All sketch maps are very approximate and you will gain more enjoyment and accuracy of route finding by using the appropriate Ordnance Survey 1:25,000 sheets.

We hope that users of this volume will enjoy the walks as much as we do when exploring this delightful area. Please remember the Country Code and have respect for the countryside and those who live and work there. Please let Lancashire County Council in Preston know of any footpath problems. We are grateful for those readers who have commented on previous editions and we hope that this one matches your aspirations.

Ian and Krysia Brodie

Walk 1

The Twin Rivers

Abbeystead – Tarnbrook – Marshaw – Abbeystead
10 Kilometres (6 Miles) (whole distance Wyre Way)
Start: Abbeystead Hamlet by the School (GR 563543)
Bus: Service 146 or 147 Lancaster to Abbeystead
Car Parking: Stoops Bridge, to the east of the school by
the riverside.
Map: O.S. Leisure Sheet 41, The Forest of Bowland

*The River Wyre rises on the fells above Abbeystead and
it is formed from two main tributaries, the Marshaw
and the Tarnbrook Wyres.*

his walk explores the dales of these two tributaries.
The whole catchment is owned by the Duke of
Westminster and is managed for shooting and agri-
culture. The moors were once said to be the most
productive grouse shoot in England, whilst the copse-
speckled landscape is designed for pheasant and rough
shooting. This walks traverses an interesting mixture of
landscape types.

❶ *Abbeystead House and its well cared for gardens are seen
from the walk near the end of the route. The area was a
medieval hunting chase – a claim that might still ring true.*

3

Walk 1: The Twin Rivers

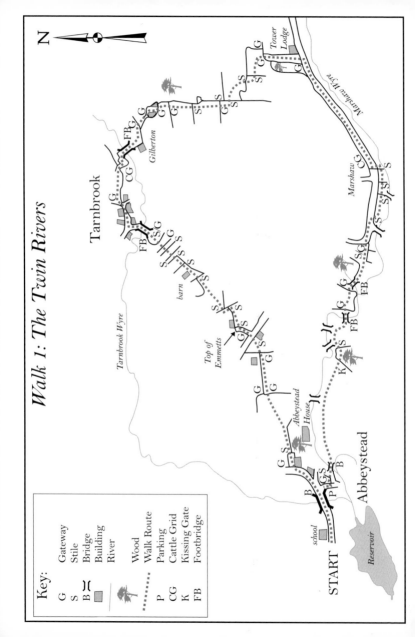

❶ *The whole walk forms the upper loop of the Wyre Way.*

⊛ With the school on your left walk down the road from the hamlet, cross Stoops Bridge over the Tarnbrook Wyre, pass the entrance lodge to Abbeystead House and then climb the road steeply uphill. When the road bends left go right through the gate adjacent to the cottage on your right and go to enter the field by the stile at the rear of the garage and garden. (600 metres)

Follow the right-hand wall and wood but when it starts to curve away to the right cross the remainder of the field by going under the overhead power lines and aiming for the farm buildings ahead. Go through the right of two gates and follow near the left-hand fence to go through the gate in the far left-hand corner. Cross the next field to reach the road by a stile found to the left of the gate-house cottage seen ahead. (900 metres)

Cross the road, go down the short access track to Top of Emmetts but just short of the yard go right, over a stile and follow the left-hand boundary, and then cross the stile in the far left-hand corner of the field. In the next field follow the right-hand boundary and, after a short distance, cross the stile to your right. (300 metres)

❶ *From the stile views of the amphitheatre of the Tarnbrook Wyre can be seen lying below the slopes of Ward's Stone Fell. To the south is the ridge of Haythornthwaite Fell.*

⊛ In the field cross the reed area towards a barn whose

5

Ouzel Thorn Farm, Tarnbrook

Pea Carr Barn and the upper reaches of the Tarnbrook Wyre

roof could be seen from the stile. On your way pick up a left-hand fence line and cross the stile in the far left-hand corner. Go past the right-hand side of the barn and then follow the right-hand fence to cross a stone stile in the far right-hand corner. In the next field follow the right-hand wall and fence, cross the stile in the field corner, bear left to cross the next stile across the access lane. (1000 metres)

Cross the middle of the next field to go over a stile in the short section of stone wall and then directly across the field to climb the stile facing you. Go down the field to cross the stile by the gate at the bottom of the field and then cross the gated bridge over the Tarnbrook Wyre. Follow the enclosed track to the Tarnbrook hamlet and turn right to go through the settlement. (380 metres)

ⓘ *The houses of the hamlet are of interest because of their vernacular features. The settlement is a 'closed' village in the Abbeystead estate but at one time it comprised 25 dwellings, of which nine housed Quaker families, and employed the skills of a hundred hatters and glovemakers. Tarnbrook was a vaccary (a farm site – see information box on page 113).*

⫪ At the far end of the hamlet go through the gate at the end of the metalled road. Continue along this farm and moorland access track, bear right at the fork, go over the cattle grid and continue to pass a second cattle grid just short of Gilberton Farm and the river. (750 metres)

ⓘ *The open area is dotted with signs to remind you that the*

7

Grit Fell above Abbeystead

moorland is private and access is restricted to a concessionary strip and footpaths. The estate zealously restricts public access and Lancashire County Council pays a tribute to the owners and provides a ranger service for the limited access. A 'Freedom to Roam' Access Act will make more of this delightful countryside accessible.

🚶 From the cattle grid go left and cross the river by the footbridge upstream from the farm bridge. Continue ahead behind the farm and turn left on a track to follow the wall – now on your right. This track takes you over two small-arched bridges, and through two gates to reach a yard between two barns. Immediately bear right in the yard to leave by the first gate. (300 metres)

Turn left in the field and follow the left-hand wall up

Abbeystead House

and then go through the gate in the top left-hand field corner. Continue upwards in the next field going parallel to the left-hand boundary and wood and cross the stile in the top left-hand field corner. Continue up in the third field and go through the prominent gate in the facing boundary. (375 metres)

Continue near the left-hand boundary, ignore the first, wooden, ladder stile but cross the next, iron, ladder stile. You are now at the highest point of the walk and on the edge of the moor. Here fields can easily revert to moorland vegetation or, with drainage and fertiliser, become grassy fields. Such is the balance of the landscape. Go half right to cross the next, shorter, ladder stile and then half left to cross the recently rebuilt wall (an excellent example of walling) by a stone stile. (500 metres)

9

Go diagonally down hill to the far right-hand corner of the field, passing the concrete bases of wartime army huts. Go through the right-hand gate between the two wood ends in the field corner. Follow the track down by the right-hand-wall and reach the road just beyond the gate at Tower Lodge. (375 metres)

Go right and follow the road until a cattle grid crosses it. (1500 metres)

❶ *This section of road known by the name of the glacial melt-water channel through which the road climbs, the Trough of Bowland, is a favourite picnicking area. Recent plantings of Scots pine are restoring the area's character.*

(🚶) On the near side of the cattle grid go over the stile on the left and follow the right-hand wall down the river-side field. Cross a small slab footbridge before crossing a stile. Continue near the right-hand wall to cross a further stile by a footbridge and then, in the next field, follow the right-hand boundary but, after 30 metres of fence beyond the walled section, cross the stile to gain access to the road side. (500 metres)

Go left on the road, ignore the left turn (to Scorton) and continue until the road bends sharp right. Enter the field ahead by the stile and gate and follow the left-hand boundary along until the wall bends away to the left. From here to the start are a number of footbridges across the Marshaw Wyre but many are marked private and are not used on the walk. From here go towards the

Tower Lodge, Marshaw

right-hand fence of the wood and follow this closely down to cross a small footbridge with the river still to your left. Pass through the subsequent gate and then follow the path by the left-hand fence until it gives way to a walled boundary. Climb the hillock to your right but return down after a short distance to a small gate and footbridge now facing you. Cross the river here. (750 metres)

Go forward in the field, climb gently to pass a sycamore with a holly behind. After passing these trees keep your height above the river and a wood above you to the left. The path gets nearer the river and then crosses a relatively level grassy area. The river then meanders left to a steep bluff. On the left is a flight of stone steps that leads you up the steep embankment to a stile and beyond you enter a short section of woodland. A stone commemorates the planting in 1908 of the wood during the ownership of Lord Sefton. Leave the wood by the kissing gate. (400 metres)

Keep near to but above the right-hand fence as you traverse this long field. You pass the front of Abbeystead House where you then descend to cross a substantial footbridge near the far end of this long field. The field often has some wet sections. Abbeystead House was built in 1886 by the Earl of Sefton and is Elizabethan in style. The windows have mullions and transoms and it cost £100,000 to build. It is what one wag calls 'a palatial shooting box'. (800 metres)

Turn left in the field and, after the wooden shelter, follow the left-hand fence and then pass through the metal rail field gate before bearing right to reach the metalled road. Turn left over Stoops Bridge to return to the start. (500 metres)

Norse names: a number of the local place names appear to have a Norse origin. Those ending in *fell* (a hill), *dale* (valley) being the most obvious. Others include *tarn* (small lake), *beck* (stream), *clough* (or *cleugh* – a ravine), and *Brock* (brocc – a badger). Grizedale is the valley of the wild pig (*griss*). Hazel-hurst Fell is the hazel wooded hillside (*hyrst*). Snape Rake Lane is the track up the hillside (from *reik*).

Walk 2

Upper Wyresdale – Once the Home of Abbots

Abbeystead – Lower Swainshead – Catshaw – Reservoir – Abbeystead

6.5 Kilometres (4 Miles) (Wyre Way 2.6 Km)
Start: Abbeystead Hamlet by the School
Bus: Service 146 or 147 Lancaster to Abbeystead
Car Parking: Stoops Bridge – to the East of the School
(GR 563543)
Map: O.S. Leisure Sheet 41 Forest of Bowland

An excellent walk downstream of Abbeystead that reflects the nature of the young River Wyre. Steep wooded bluffs, riverside fields, and dramatic wooded cloughs tumbling down to the river. This walk, and Walk 16, The Shepherd's Church of Wyresdale, pass a number of the interesting sculpted waymark stones. For those interested in wildlife the reservoir adds a further dimension and its architecture provides another focus of interest.

From the centre of the hamlet leave by the road to Lancaster, with the school on your right. Walk past the telephone box and climb the hill with views of the reservoir

13

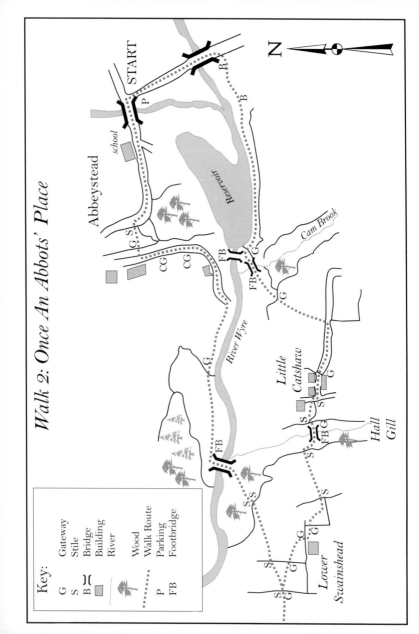

Walk 2: Once An Abbots' Place

Key:

G — Gateway
S — Stile
B — Bridge
☐ — Building
~ — River
🌲 — Wood
••• — Walk Route
P — Parking
FB — Footbridge

N

START

P

Abbeystead

school

Reservoir

Cam Brook

River Wyre

FB

FB

G S

CG CG

G

FB

G

Little Catshaw

Hall Gill

FB B

S S

Lower Swainshead

S S G G

G G

down to your left. As the hill eases the road turns right and you cross the stile by a footpath sign on your left. Cross the field towards the left-hand building and pass through the obvious gate facing you. Beyond, turn left down the concrete road to pass over two cattle grids. (750 metres)

Just after the second cattle grid the road meanders right but your route is to follow the left-hand wall down to meet the road near the stone structures that hold underground buildings. Rejoin the road and follow it past the structures with the River Wyre down to your left and, when the road bends down left, continue ahead on a track to pass through a gate. (500 metres)

The next field is a long and narrow one. Follow the track ahead but when it bends to the right continue straight ahead on the ground slightly raised above the river. The path then goes down to the left-hand river-side fence passing a carved waymark stone (fish). When the river bends away from the left-hand fence go diagonally up the slightly higher ground, pass a further stone (a duck), and then continue towards the

Wayside carving

15

end of the narrowing field. Just before the field ends the metal Long Bridge enables you to cross the River Wyre. (550 metres)

Turn right to climb from the bridge and continue right at the path junction. The clear path goes through newly planted trees in Mark Holme Wood before climbing diagonally up the wooded bluff and away from the river. Leave the wood by the second stile, after the gate. Contour ahead in the field, with Lower Swainshead Farm up to your left, but when a lone barn comes into view walk towards this to find a stile you cross in the fence ahead, and then continue in the same direction to a stile by a gate. The Wyre Way continues from here in Walk 3. (800 metres)

To return to Abbeystead put your back to the nearside of this gate and stile and go diagonally up the field and towards the left of Lower Swainshead Farm. Pass through a gateway (in the same fence that you have just crossed by a stile) and then head for the right-hand boundary. Go through the gate in the right-hand wall to enter the far side of the farmyard but then turn left and leave the track by going through the left-hand gate. Go along the long field and make for the far, top right-hand corner. Cross the double stile just beyond the right-hand gate. Continue up the next field in the direction of Haythornthwaite Fell until you pass through a gap in the remains of an earthen bank, formerly a hedge line. Bear slightly to your left and cross over the field towards some trees with some parts of farm buildings showing behind. This leads you to a stile that you cross

16

in a fence at the edge of the wood, but remains unseen until you are nearly there. (750 metres)

Follow the path diagonally right down the wooded clough and cross the footbridge over Hall Gill. Climb to the left to follow the path to a small gate and then cross the stile to your immediate left. In the field turn right and go up by the unsightly storage tank and go to cross the fence to the left of the pole-mounted electricity transformer and gain the farm access road. (300 metres)

Turn right on the road but branch immediately left to reach the yard of Little Catshaw Farm. Continue through the gated yard and on the track beyond. Follow this track until, shortly before it bends to the right, you come to a right-hand waymark stone (a ram) where the field has opened out to your right. Leave the track here by turning left into the field and follow the discontinuous line of haw-thorns (a former hedge line) to pass through a gate by the wood corner. In the next field descend sharply, initially by the right-hand fence, to go down to cross a footbridge over Cam Clough near where it joins the River Wyre. The path then goes along the riverbank to a kissing gate and an iron footbridge over the river. (1100 metres)

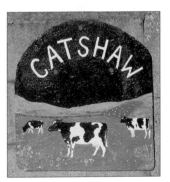

ℹ️ *Our way does not cross the river but joins a further link section of the Wyre Way that*

Spillway at Abbeystead Reservoir

goes through the small gate immediately following the kissing gate. However those with time to explore may wish to cross the bridge and explore the area around the dam to Abbeystead Reservoir, with its fish pass ladder, the grotto-like draw well and the superb spillway where overflowing water makes a delightful sound. Return across the bridge to continue.

From the small gate the path climbs up, and gives superb views of the spillway and keeps between the reservoir and the boundary wall. Later these give way to a wire fence and the wet areas near the river. The clear, but sometimes wet, path leads all the way to the road. Go left on the road and then left again over Stoops Bridge to return to Abbeystead. (1500 metres)

Walk 3

Nether Wyresdale – by Fell and Dale

Scorton – Harrisend Fell – Dolphinholme – Scorton

16 Kilometres (10 Miles) (Wyre Way 7.6 Km)
Start: Scorton Village Centre (GR502488)
Bus: Service 213 Garstang to Scorton or services 146 and
147 Lancaster to Dolphinholme and Abbeystead
Car Parking: Centre of village but this can be congested.
There is some space, on the route, just north of the bridge
over the M6 (GR 505494)
Map: O.S. Leisure Series 41 Forest of Bowland

his walk explores both the moorland edge and the
middle Wyre valley. It is a walk of contrasts and
deserves a clear day to enjoy the views. The contrast
between the river of the dipper, the rich field pattern and
the open fell of curlew and grouse all contribute to the
delights of the walk.

Leave Scorton village centre and walk along the road
towards the Trough of Bowland and leave the houses
behind. Continue over the motorway bridge and along
until the road descends, bends sharp left and crosses a
stream. Leave the road by the stile on the right (footpath
sign Harris End Fell Road) and then go to cross the

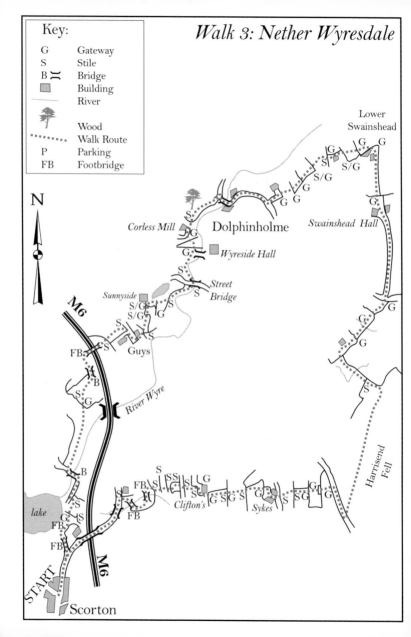

stream by the footbridge. Follow the stream on your left, with a wood on your right and re-cross the stream at the next footbridge. (1200 metres)

The path now crosses a series of good stiles. Bear right after the footbridge and cross the obvious stile in the fence. Go ahead to cross two fields and two further stiles with the stream down to your right. A third stile to cross has taken you away from the stream. In the next field bear half right and leave this field by a stile in the far left-hand corner. This leads to a road which you cross diagonally right and enter a field by a further stile. Go up the field to cross a stile to the left of Cliftons Farm buildings. Turn right and follow the gated track into the farmyard and to the front of the farmhouse. (750 metres)

With the farmhouse on your left go through the field gate, go up the field by the left-hand fence and then cross the stile by the gate facing you by the left-hand field corner. Go directly ahead up a small rise to pass to the right of a stunted oak tree. From this rise in the field there are extensive views of Morecambe Bay, the Lakeland fells and the area of your walk. Descend the rise aiming for the left-hand side of the farm buildings and cross the stile to the right of the junction of field boundaries ahead. In the next field follow near the left-hand boundary and enter the farmyard of Sykes Farm by the gate between the two outer buildings. Go right through the yard and left past the house to reach a road. (900 metres)

Cross the road directly to cross a stile and in the field

go just left of straight ahead to cross a stile in the fence facing you. Follow the left-hand fence up the field and leave by the gate in the boundary ahead. Go up the next field parallel to the right-hand boundary and look for an old iron gate which leads to a small enclosure with a stile by a gate just beyond which takes you onto rough fell land. Go half right near the main left-hand stream to reach the fell road by the footpath sign. (800 metres)

Technically your way goes right, up the road until a crest is reached with footpaths leading off on both sides of the road. Your way lies to the left and you follow the waymarked and generally distinct path across the fell side. When there is a freedom to roam you can avoid the road walking by crossing the road directly from the footpath sign and climbing just left of a direct line up the facing slope to intersect the traversing path. This path is followed left over the moorland edge until it meets a fence corner by a footpath junction. (1900 metres)

Turn left at this corner and go down the un-enclosed fell land with the fence on your right. Cross the stile in the bottom right-hand corner and then go ahead down a track, cross the small stream and continue along the track to a track junction. Go right, through the gate to arrive at the derelict Lane Head Farm. Continue along the line of the old track (still a partially enclosed lane) over a stream, up a sunken lane to a second derelict house. The track continues (once hedged on both sides), begins to bend left, goes down to cross a stream, gently climbs to a gate, beyond which you go through the further gate to arrive at the road. (800 metres)

Cross the road directly and go down the tarmac-adamed lane (Waste Lane) to the yard of Swainshead Hall Farm. Pass through the gated yard and continue, via the left-hand of two gates, down the track to reach Lower Swainshead Farm. When the track goes left into the yard beyond the house go through the gate in the wall ahead. Go left in the field, pass through a gateway in the fence below the farm and descend slightly across the next field to reach a gate and stile across your way. (2000 metres) From here back to Scorton is the Wyre Way.

Go over the stile by the gate and cross the field towards the right-hand side of the barn ahead. From the barn follow the right-hand fence and cross the next stile by the gate in the right-hand field corner. Follow the short section of right-hand wall, at the end of which you bear left aiming for Dolphinhome Village, and contour through the field to cross a further stile by a gate. Follow the left-hand fence to pass through a gate in the far left-hand corner. Take the track ahead and go down the field towards Dolphinholme House Farm. Above the house go ahead up the short farm access track to the road. Follow the road right and eventually down to the bridge over the River Wyre in Lower Dolphinholme. (2000 metres)

❶ *On the building on the left before the bridge is a restored old gas lamp testimony to the fact that Dolphinholme Mill, a worsted mill of 1787, was one of the first in the country to be illuminated by gas lights. It employed a thousand spinners and wool was combed in houses. The mill warehouse (1797) just over the bridge is now a terrace of four houses.*

🚶 Cross the bridge and just above the houses turn left off the road and take the lower of two paths to pass the sewage treatment plant and go along a path with the wood on your right and, after a bend, a wall on your left. Follow this path for its full length, cross the stile ahead and then cross the field aiming for the left-hand side of the white farmhouse. Go into the farmyard by the small gate adjacent to the house with the former water wheel of Corless Mill to your left. This old corn

Ward's Stone and Wyresdale from Harrisend Fell

mill displays the seventeen-foot diameter, five-foot wide waterwheel, two millstones and a cottage with a curious-shaped roof. The gothic windows of the house add to the character. (800 metres)

Continue along the farm access track, past the cottage and climb up the track with the river down to your left. As the track climbs look for a small gateway on your left that leads you along a path through a small wood and then by a small gate into the field. Follow the left-hand riverbank path, pass the bridge to Wyreside Hall, and continue along the riverbank for about 60 metres. Turn right to reach the road by a stile. The neglected bridge gave access to Wyreside Hall. The house, dated 1852, with its dark grey stone, giant pilaster and porch of fluted ionic columns is well sited to enjoy views of the river valley. (500 metres)

Turn left on the road (take great care) and then turn right to cross the stile at the near end of Street Bridge. Continue along the riverbank path and eventually cross a ladder stile on your right to gain access to a track at the end of the fishing lake. Go left on the track to reach the nearside of the house, Sunnyside. At the edge of the house garden turn left to cross a ladder stile by the gate in the corner. In the field go half right and along to a further ladder stile by a gate in the right-hand boundary. Turn left in this next field and follow the stream down until the hedgerow crosses to your side of the ditch bank. From here cross the remainder of the field towards the left-hand corner of the buildings ahead. Guys Farm is now a Girl Guide camp.

Cross the stile near the buildings, go down the left-hand side of these buildings and then turn right onto the track that passes the front of the house. (1200 metres)

Take the first track left (towards Nan Kings – a farmyard with many activities) but turn immediately right to enter the field by a stile. Turn left in the field and go to cross the footbridge over the motorway, after crossing a stile and a small stream across your path before the bridge is reached. Across the M6 turn left and go down into the lower field. Cross the dyke by the bridge and then turn right and follow the dyke side and following fence to reach a gate and stile at the far end of the field. Cross the stile and follow the distinct path, near the riverbank, to the road at Cleveley Bridge. (1400 metres)

Turn left over the bridge and then right over a stile by a gate (footpath sign Park Lane). Follow this track until it climbs up to top a small embankment. Leave the track by crossing the stile on your left going into the field and then almost immediately turning right into a path with poor wire fencing on either side. Follow this narrow, enclosed path and cross over the corner of the field to find the old mill race on your right. Follow the race until your path crosses the end of a right-angled ditch. Now cross the remainder of the field directly to a gate and stile behind the prominent tin shed. Over the stile go ahead to cross the footbridge on your right, follow the enclosed path along and, after a further footbridge, you come to the road. Scorton is to the right. (1700 metres)

Walk 4

Nicky Nook – a Perennial Favourite

Garstang – Grizedale- Nicky Nook – Scorton – Gartsang

11.5 kilometres (7 miles) (Wyre Way 4 kilometres)
Start: Garstang Discovery Centre (GR 493454)
Bus: Garstang is served by regular services from
Lancaster, Preston and Blackpool (Services 40, 41, X42, and 42)
Car Parking: By Garstang Discovery Centre.
Map: O.S. Outdoor Leisure 41 Forest of Bowland

This is the classic route for walkers from Garstang
despite the need to use sections of country lanes. It
encompasses a feeling of the local fells, woodlands and
water – elements which combine to make our countryside so attractive.

From the Discovery Centre go through the rear car
park to the river and follow it along the sports field
edge path along the river and climb the steps up the
near side of the bridge abutment. (370 metres) The
bridge crosses the extraction point from the Lune–Wyre
Conjunctive Use Scheme; from here water supplies are
piped to the Frank Law Treatment works at Catterall
before joining the North West supply grid. (The

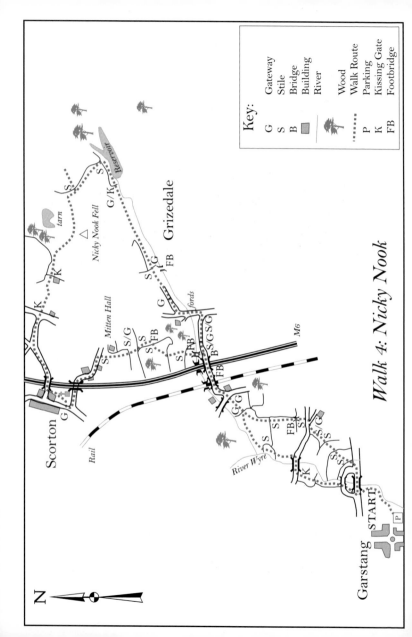

Key:

G	Gateway
S	Stile
B	Bridge
	Building
	River
	Wood
	Walk Route
P	Parking
K	Kissing Gate
FB	Footbridge

Walk 4: Nicky Nook

Scorton

Grizedale

Garstang

START

River Wyre

Nicky Nook Fell

Mitten Hall

Reservoir

tarn

M6

Rail

N

Grizedale Lea Reservoir

upstream barriers are to prevent flood-waters from inundating villages down stream.)

Go over the bridge and just after the embankment track has joined from the left go down to cross a stile and then across the field to a further stile. In the next field continue in the same direction to cross a further stile near the right-hand field corner. Go across the next field to the left-hand boundary, which is followed to a stile by a gate, and access to Wyre Lane. (500 metres)

Go right along the lane, bear left at the junction and immediately over the bridge go over the stile on your left. Cross the middle of the field (often very wet and needing a detour) to cross the footbridge in the facing hedge. Follow the right-hand fence in the next field, go over the stile in the far right-hand corner and continue along the fence line until it bends away to your right. (500 metres)

Bear right here and go through the kissing gate by a gate to the left of the wood. Keep near the stream but then go directly to pass through the gate in the section of stone wall at the far end of the field. Cross the road diagonally right and go down the short track to the left of the industrial buildings to reach the railway. (750 metres)

Cross the railway footbridge and subsequent motorway bridge and continue ahead to cross a stile by a gate by the right-hand corner of a wood. Follow the track along with the wood on your left down to a stile and gate and the metalled lane beyond. Go left down the lane that crosses two streams, past the entrance to Throstle Nest farm on your left, and, as the road starts to climb,

Looking North from Nicky Nook

a track signed as a bridlepath goes off to your right. (1100 metres)

Go down this track, through the gate and continue along the beck-side path to a further gate and stile (with a footbridge to your right). Go over the stile and continue along the definite track as it climbs up the dale to arrive, after a further gate and kissing gate, at Grizedale reservoir. (1700 metres)

ⓘ *Grizedale was damned in 1861–63. Whilst the waters are too acidic to be able to support much life it is not without its interests. Grizedale is Norse for valley of the wild pigs.*

ⓧ Continue along the track until almost opposite the fork in the reservoir there is a break in the left-hand fence that gives access to a stile in the wall with a footpath sign to Scorton and Nicky Nook. Cross the stile and climb the steep path that keeps near the right-hand fence and wall until, on the top area, a ladder stile crosses the wall. Do not cross but turn left and take the path that climbs gently to the triangulation point on the fell top at a height of 215 metres. (850 metres)

ⓘ *The fell offers extensive views of the Forest of Bowland moors, the Lakeland fells, the Fylde plain and Morecambe Bay. On clear days the Isle of Man and North Wales can be seen. The spread of rhododendron and the state of some of the walls on parts of the fell cry out for attention.*

Stake House Fell from Nicky Nook Fell

(🚶) Continue along the ridge heading towards Morecambe Bay as the path leads down and right towards the pine trees above the topmost tarn. From here the right-hand wall and fence lead down to a kissing gate above a small reservoir and then more steeply down to a stile to the right of a house at a road junction. Follow the road directly ahead all the way down to Scorton. (2000 metres)

(🛈) *Scorton is an attractive village with the older properties built of the local gritstone. Refreshments and toilets are available but the village is often busy with tourists at weekends.*

(🚶) From the bottom of Snowhill (the road you used to enter the village) turn by the war memorial and school and walk down the driveway to the church. Go through the lychgate to the church grounds – the building of 1878-79 is a typical solid stone design of Paley and Austin reflecting Victorian values, and cost £14,000 to build. Just beyond the tower turn right through a small gate and descend the field, past a huge oak tree, to a further gate and the road. (270 metres)

Turn left on the road and, just after the tennis and bowling club, left again into Tithebarn Lane. Go under the M6 and continue to pass a group of houses on the left-hand bend. After the last house on the right, East Barn, go up the road to find a stile in the hedge above the top of the garden. The Wyre Way sign points us to Hazelhead Lane. (550 metres)

In the field cross parallel to the M6 and pick up the left-hand boundary that passes the house – Mitton Hall – and leads to a gateway and stile in the far left-hand corner. Now aim for the stile to the left of the corner of the wood ahead. Over this stile follow the right-hand fence of the wood to a footbridge and stile that allows you to enter the wood. Turn left and follow the track through the wood to a gate and stile on its left. (900 metres)

Cross the stile and go towards the right-hand corner of the field and M6 to find a stile and then a path through the gorse that goes over a footbridge. Zigzag up the embankment, go over the motorway and railway bridges and then ahead to the road. Cross the road and go through the gate ahead with its Wyre Way footpath sign. (300 metres)

Go down the field to pass through the kissing gate

Grizedale

and gate to the right of the wood and then follow the right-hand stream down to the River Wyre. Turn left and climb the slight rise of Broom Hill, a much-eroded small drumlin, and then descend to cross two stiles and regain the riverside path. Go along to pass the aqueduct and then go over the footbridge and along to Wyre Lane. (1000 metres)

Cross the lane to a kissing gate and follow the path along to a further kissing gate by a wooden sculpture of a dipper. The surfaced path follows the riverbank via a stepped embankment and enables you to continue to your starting point in Garstang. (1000 metres)

❶ *For a shorter route, but missing out a section of the Wyre Way, the walk can be started at Scorton and the section from Garstang to the M6 at Woodacre can be omitted.*

The name BOWLAND, more correctly pronounced as BOLLAND, translates as the 'land of the cattle' – a reference to the urus, the wild cattle present in the wilder parts of Britain in pre-Roman days.

Walk 5

Garstang, Churchtown, St Michael's and Nateby

Garstang – Churchtown – St Michael's – Nateby – Garstang
15.2 Kilometres (9.5 Miles) (Wyre Way 6.25 Km)
Start: Garstang Discovery Centre (GR 493454)
Bus: See Walk 4
Car Parking: As Walk 4
O.S. Map Pathfinder 668 Garstang

his walk follows the Wyre Way downstream from Garstang to Churchtown and on to St Michael's-on-Wyre. If walkers want a circular route back to Garstang the walk suggested crosses the former mosslands on the Fylde and whilst few contour lines are crossed the fieldpaths can be wet after rainfall. In some cases the stiles are not as easy to cross as should be desirable. The route offers excellent views back to the fells of the Forest of Bowland.

Go down the side of the Garstang Discovery Centre, across the car park to reach the riverbank. Turn right and follow the Wyre downstream on a tarmac path that eventually leads out on to the High Street. Turn left

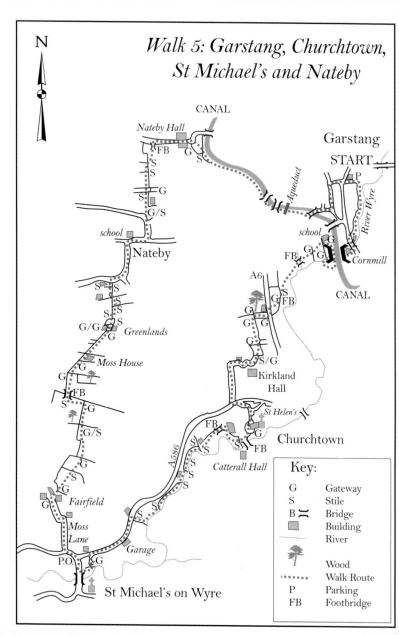

Walk 5: Garstang, Churchtown, St Michael's and Nateby

N

CANAL

Nateby Hall

Garstang

START

P

FB

G

S

S

Aqueduct

River Wyre

S

G

S

G/S

school

CANAL

school

G

G

FB

G

G

Cornmill

Nateby

A6

S

G

FB

G

S

S

S

S

G

G

S

G/G

Greenlands

G

S/G

Kirkland
Hall

Moss House

G

G

G

FB

St Helen's

S

G

FB

FB

G

S

G/S

Churchtown

S

Catterall Hall

G

A586

S

S

S

G

S

S

Fairfield

G

Moss
Lane

Garage

P.O.

G

St Michael's on Wyre

Key:

G   Gateway

S   Stile

B ⟩⟨   Bridge

[building] Building

        River

[tree] Wood

...... Walk Route

P   Parking

FB   Footbridge

and cross the bridge over the river but then immediately cross the road and go down the short access to the Cornmill Nursing Home. (500 metres)

Pass under the archway of the building and go along the track that once followed the millrace and then pass under the aqueduct by the riverside. Climb the steps on the far side and reach the canal towpath. Cross over the aqueduct, the canal to your right, and walk along until the fence on your left gives way to a hedge. You are almost level with the Tithebarn canal basin. Leave the towpath through the small gate and cross the school field to pass through a kissing gate. (350 metres) The path is called Many Pads and was the main route to St Helen's at Churchtown, once the Parish Church for Garstang.

Cross the next field to pass through the next kissing gate and then cross the field to a stiled footbridge. The riverbank is now close to your left and this is followed until the river

High Street, Garstang

37

bends left. From here make right across the field to aim for the farm. (These fields may be developed soon for housing.) Cross a further stiled footbridge and then climb the bank to reach the busy A6 road by a small gate. (600 metres)

Go left on the A6 verge but then carefully cross the road to arrive by the far end of the farm buildings. Go through the gated farmyard along a concrete track, continue to follow this alongside a wood until it meets two adjacent gates. Go through the left-hand gate and follow the track along the left-hand field boundary until it bends left at the end of the field. Go through the gate facing you and then cross the next field directly to a gate and stile in the far right-hand corner near the rear of Kirkland Hall to find a track. Turn right along this track, pass the rear of the hall, Keepers' Cottage and Kirkland Hall Farm and then continue along the farm access road as it bends left to reach the main road just outside Churchtown. (1750 metres)

❶ *Kirkland Hall has a seven-bay, two-and-a-half storey brick façade built in 1760, but the rear wings contain some seventeenth-century brickwork and date-stones from 1668 and 1695. The Butlers, whose home this once was, were adherents to the House of Stuart and when the King's forces captured Kirkland Hall they took Alexander Butler and his servant as prisoners, on horseback, to Preston. On the journey the servant slipped from his horse and unseated his master into a ditch. The troopers found him more dead than alive and left him* *to his fate. However, he recovered, remounted and returned home.*

🏃 Cross the A586 to the left and then go through the middle of the village, passing the market cross and the Punchbowl Inn to reach St Helen's Church. Continue through the car park and graveyard extension to reach a small gate by a seat. (500 metres)

ℹ️ *St Helen's claims the title of the 'Cathedral of the Fylde' and this large church is full of interest. Some of the stonework is twelfth century and the circular nature of the original churchyard suggests it was an earlier, pagan site. The interior has an elaborate carved pulpit of 1646, oak beams donated by*

St Helen's, Churchtown

Henry IV from his nearby Myerscough hunting chase, and rudely carved miserichords from Cockersand Abbey (see walk 14). The church tower is fifteenth century and the yard has some plague gravestones and two, with carvings showing people in prayer, are referred to as Adam and Eve. The river once lapped by the church and it has been suggested that the church owes its origin to Celtic missionaries who came up the river by coracle.

Ⓚ Follow the embankment towards the footbridge (built in 1985 to replace the suspension bridge washed away in 1980) and Catterall Hall, one of the oldest Wyreside houses, on the far bank. Do not cross the river but continue downstream and cross a stile at the far end of the field. Continue along the bank-side path and follow the right-hand fence of the sewage works around to cross a footbridge over a tributary stream. Follow the right-hand hedge across the next field and then go to cross a stile in the boundary directly ahead. (600 metres)

From now, until we rejoin the road, the path is a permissive footpath. Over the stile, with the river again directly to your left, continue to follow the right-hand fence (ignoring the right-hand stile at the start) until a stile crosses your way. Over the stile continue to follow the right-hand fence until the next stile. Continue along the path near the riverbank and after a section with the fence on your left the path again follows a right-hand fence, goes around a short section of tributary stream, again follows the riverbank and then drops down to a stile on your right opposite a white house. Cross this stile, go along the left-hand side of the narrow field and gain the road by a stile by a gate. Go left along the verge and then roadside footway, go past the garage, pass The Oaks until you are almost opposite Mallards Restaurant in St Michael's-on-Wyre. (1600 metres)

Turn left down Allotment Road and follow this straight road until it goes left. Your way lies ahead through the gate. A short distance further brings you to the riverbank and the path is followed to the right to reach the main road where it crosses the river to reach the church. The Wyre Way continues ahead here but our route back to Garstang turns right along the road to pass the Grapes Inn. (350 metres)

Cross the main road from the Grapes and continue to the road junction by the Post Office. Turn left (signposted Out Rawcliffe), pass Paddington Avenue but then cross the road to the right and go down Moss Lane. This access road (cul-de-sac) is followed all the way along until the surfaced lane ends at Fairfield Farm. (1300 metres)

On entering the farm pass the bungalow and first two buildings on your right and then turn right on the gated track between the farm buildings. Continue on this track as it bends left and enters a field. Leave the track here by turning right to cross the field parallel to the left-hand fence to cross a stile in the patchy hedge facing you.

41

Cross the next field to go through the obvious gate directly ahead. This leads to a track which you cross to enter a large field. Follow the left-hand hedge, cross through the gate by the stile in the far left-hand field corner, with a wood to the left, and then continue along the left-hand boundary for the length of the next field. In the far left-hand corner turn left to go through the gate and then follow the right-hand hedge until it bends right towards the right-hand field corner. Cross the right-hand stile, some 30 metres short of the field corner, and subsequent footbridge over Pilling Water into the next field. (1200 metres)

ⓘ *These large, flat, regular-shaped fields that once were moss-land give extensive views east to the hills of the Forest of Bowland.*

ⓧ In this next field follow the left-hand hedge, pass through the gate in the far left-hand corner and then continue along by the left-hand boundary towards Moss House Farm. Go through the gate facing you in the left-hand field corner and then use the track ahead which skirts the left-hand side of the farm buildings. Continue along the straight farm access road, ignore the left turn and go straight to the gate that leads to the yard of the former farm, now a house, called Greenlands. (1000 metres)

Go through the gate and continue straight ahead to leave the enclosed area by two consecutive gates just to the right of the outbuilding. Cross the small paddock and go directly ahead to cross a stile and then cross the stile to your immediate right. In this next field turn to follow the left-hand boundary to cross the stile in the far left-hand corner. Continue along the left-hand boundary in the next field and cross a further stile, on your left, in the far left-hand field corner. Go right in this next area to follow near the right-hand boundary up past a menage and then down to cross a stile in the far right-hand field corner. Go through the short woodland and gain the road by a further stile. (700 metres)

Turn right down the road and follow the main Garstang road passing the school, post office until, at the far side of Nateby village, a road to Pilling, Kilcrash Lane, goes left. Go down this lane until it bends left. Cross the stile by the gate facing you and then cross the field to pick up the right-hand boundary by the bunga-low. Cross the stile in the far right-hand field corner, go right on the concrete road but turn left into the field just before the gate over the track. (1300 metres) Beyond the farm is Bowers House, now a restaurant, dated 1627 with a room once used as a Roman Catholic chapel or oratory. There were once rumours of a secret passage from here to Nateby Hall Farm.

Follow the right-hand field boundary and cross the stile ahead to continue on the path through the small wood and leave by a concrete stile that once marked the old Pilling Pig railway line. Continue by the left-hand boundary down the next field but, when the boundary

Nateby Hall Bridge

bends left after a clump of trees, cross the remainder of the field by aiming for a stile in line with the trees to the left of the farm buildings. Cross the stile and subsequent footbridge and then go right along the track to the yard of Nateby Hall Farm. The original hall was destroyed by fire in 1870. Go through the farmyard and as the access track leaves and bends left go to your right through the double gate into a triangular field. Go right and up the field towards the concrete blocks, pass between these and gain the canal towpath by a stile above the ruinous lime-kiln. The kiln once burned lime-stone brought down the canal from the Kendal area for use on the local fields. (1100 metres)

To return to Garstang and your starting place go right along the canal towpath, pass the marina on your left, go under two road bridges and one pipe bridge, and then leave the canal by the next bridge. Go over the bridge and follow the road back to the centre of Garstang and to the Discovery Centre. (2350 metres)

Visitor Centres: If you wish to acquire more information about the landscapes and wildlife you might see on the walks then Wyre Borough Council operates two centres. There is the Discovery Centre, High Street Garstang (01995 602125) and the Wyreside Ecology Centre at Stanah on the Wyre Estuary (01253 857890).

Useful Addresses: (a) For footpath problems contact the footpath section of Lancashire County Council County Surveyors Dept, Guild House, Cross Street, Preston, PR1 8RD
(b) For countryside matters contact the Lancashire Branch of the Council for the Protection of Rural England, Derby Wing, Worden Hall, Worden Park, Leyland, Preston, PR5 2DJ. (c) For wildlife matters contact the Lancashire Wildlife Trust, Cuerden Park Wildlife Centre, Bamber Bridge, Preston, PR5 6AU. (d) The Ramblers' Association Mid-Lancashire local contact is David Kelly, 4 Buttermere Close, Bamber Bridge, Preston, PR5 4RT.

Walk 6

St Michael's-on-Wyre, Out Rawcliffe, Great Eccleston

St Michael's–on-Wyre – Out Rawcliffe – Great Eccleston – St Michael's.

12.3 Kilometres (7.75 Miles) (Wyre Way: 6.5 Km)
Start: St Michael's-on-Wyre Parish Church (GR 462409)
Bus: Garstang to Poulton and Blackpool 42 & X42 Services
Cars: There is a car park just around from the Church in Hall Lane.

Map: O.S. Pathfinder 668 Garstang

---

his walk uses a number of less frequented footpaths on the Fylde and a number of bird species can often be seen. Choose a quiet, sunny winter day with Cumulus clouds adding a skyscape to the open views and the fine landscape towards the Forest of Bowland. An area that gives you a perception of being wooded but the few small woods and the hedgerow trees are actually very thin on the ground.

❶ *The authors believe this is the poorest section of the Wyre Way as it rarely sees the river. However, more of the river can be appreciated on our return route. St Michael's Church*

Walk 6: St Michael, Great Eccleston and Out Rawcliffe

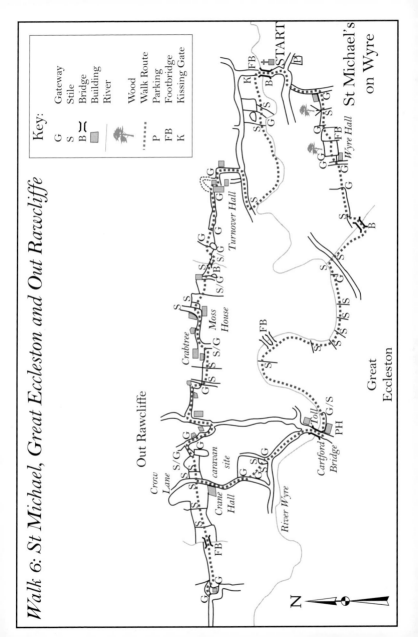

Key:

G — Gateway
S — Stile
B — Bridge
■ — Building
🌲 — River

····· Wood
····· Walk Route
P — Parking
FB — Footbridge
K — Kissing Gate

START

St Michael's on Wyre

Wyre Hall

Turnover Hall

Out Rawcliffe

Crow Lane

Crane Hall

caravan site

Crabtree

Moss House

Toll

Cartford Bridge

PH

Great Eccleston

River Wyre

N

was said to have existed in 640 and was mentioned in the Domesday Survey of 1086. It was rebuilt in 1525 and the church is possibly a mixture of thirteenth-, fifteenth- and sixteenth-century parts.

(🕿) From St Michael's Church cross the River Wyre by the footbridge and on the far bank turn immediately left, cross the road with care, and enter the riverside field by a kissing gate (Wyre Way sign to Rawcliffe Road). Follow the riverbank along the embankment top, over a stile, pass the fishing lakes, through a kissing gate, eventually over a further stile and then a final stile gives access to Rawcliffe Road. Turn right along the road and go to the second driveway on the left to Turnover Hall Farm. (1500 metres)

Go down the farm access road (Wyre Way sign to Lancaster Road) which bends left after the bungalow. Go straight ahead through the farmyard (often very messy, gated and not very rambler friendly) until a range of outbuildings blocks your way and with the house down to the left. Turn right here, go through the gate and then turn immediately left to pass the last buildings and leave the yard on a track through a gate. Ignore the track to the right as you continue along a straight track that eventually leads into a field by a gate. (650 metres)

Go along the field near the left-hand boundary and leave by the small gate in the left-hand corner of the field and adjacent to the pond on your left. Continue ahead to pick up the left-hand boundary but cross this at a stile by a gate. Turn right in the next field, to continue towards the tower silo, go over a further stile by a gate but on a bridge, and then aim for the left-hand of two gates in line with the building adjacent to the silo. Wildboar Farm lies to your right. Pass through this gate, go diagonally left across the farm access track and then enter the field to pass the silo on its immediate left. (650 metres)

Leave this field by a stile and gate to the left-hand side of the storage tank in the right-hand field corner. In the next field cross directly to the building to the right of the bungalow and cross two stiles in succession to gain a farm access road. Bear left and then follow the straight track, pass Fir Tree farm (kennels) and go towards the yard of Crabtree Farm. Do not enter the yard but turn left on the access road, and immediately go over the stile by the gate on your right-hand side to re-enter a field. (700 metres)

Follow the right-hand field boundary, pass the farm-house, and then leave the field by crossing the stile facing you in the far right-hand corner. Continue by the right-hand boundary in the next field and leave it by a further stile in the boundary across your way. Go right on the access track but immediately leave this through the gate on your left. Follow this short former access road but, opposite the house, turn left at the track junction. Follow this track past Bowland House and all the way along to the road. (1000 metres)

Go left on the road and, after about 200 metres,

turn right along Sandy Lane. (Wyre Way sign Crook Gate Lane) This track goes past a property, two semi-detached cottages, under an overhead power line with a pole-mounted transformer and through a gate. Immediately through the gate turn left through the adjacent gate, go along a short enclosed green track to a stile, through the gate at the far end and go into a field. Cross the field to find a stile mid-way between two over-head power line poles and then cross the shorter next field to a prominent stile that gives you access to Crow Lane. (1250 metres)

❶ *The circular walk and the Wyre Way route part here to avoid road walking on the return route. If you want to walk the whole Wyre Way in loops then follow the instructions in the next paragraph and return to this point.*

🚶 Directly cross Crow Lane and the subsequent stile and go down the field aiming to the left of the small wood ahead. Cross the stile in the fence facing you and go down the next field parallel to the right-hand boundary and cross the prominent stile ahead. Continue towards a prominent hedge to cross the next field that you leave by a small footbridge. In the next field follow the right-hand hedge all the way to the gate in the top right-hand corner. Through this gate bear left behind the house and reach the road through a gate. (900 metres) Go left down the road to the riverbank and the Wyre Way description continues in Walk 7.

To continue the circular walk turn left down the green track of Crow Lane and continue down the facing farm access track when, shortly, you reach Crane Hall Farm. This access road is followed past the caravan site and wood on your left. Go through the second gate on your left to enter the left-hand field. Cross the field towards a small triangular wood and then cross two consecutive stiles to emerge by the gateway to Rawcliffe Hall. Go right through the gate and then left on the road to follow the River Wyre along to the toll paying (pedestrians are free) Cartford Bridge. Cross the bridge. (1600 metres)

Immediately over the bridge turn left on a track on the near side of the Cartford Hotel and continue to follow the top of the riverside embankment. This leads over a stile by a gate, goes over a further stile, passes an aqueduct and adjacent footbridge (do not cross) and then continues by five further stiles and a gateway. Beyond this continue to cross a further stile and join the main A586 Great Eccleston–St Michael's Road where a small tributary drain joins the Wyre. (2750 metres) The village of Great Eccleston could be reached by any of the paths leading right from the embankment.

Cross the road with care and then the subsequent stile. Continue along the drain-side embankment until it is bridged. Cross the bridge and then walk diagonally left to cross a stile where the left-hand fence kinks. Follow the right-hand boundary and then pass through the gate facing you in the far right-hand corner of the field. Cross the next field to go through the gate seen by the white-painted Wyre Hall. (800 metres)

After the gate go diagonally left to cross an access track to enter a field, that faces the front of the house, by the gate. Walk by the right-hand boundary and through the gate facing you. Go down this long field parallel to the left-hand wood, cross the footbridge in the boundary facing you, and cross the next field so as to pass through the gate in the far left-hand corner. Cross the adjacent track, pass through the small unfenced copse and then follow the left-hand ditch along the edge of the field. Cross the stile in the left-hand field corner and continue along the left-hand boundary to pass through the gate facing you. Turn left down the lane to reach the main road and your starting point is to the right. (1400 metres)

The Wyre Way is the creation of Wyre Borough Council Countryside Service. They have two leaflets available on the route which, they suggest is a 41-mile walking route and is covered in three sections. These are Fleetwood to Knott End at 16 miles (our Walks 9 and 8 cover this section); Shard Bridge to Garstang as 10 miles (our Walks 5, 6 and 7) and Garstang to Tarnbrook/Marshaw as 15 miles (our Walks 1, 2, 3 and 4). The routes in this book cover the route from the source down to the sea.

The Way has much to commend it with the river passing through differing landscapes and with a variety of wildlife – especially birds – to see. Copies of the leaflet can be obtained from Wyre Borough Council.

Walk 7

Hambleton, Out Rawcliffe, Aldwath

Hambleton – Out Rawcliffe – Aldwath – Hambleton
11.6 kilometres (7 miles) –Wyre Way 4.4 Km
Start: Centre of Hambleton Village by The Shovels Public
House (GR 371424)
Bus: 88 Lancaster to Fleetwood or 89 Lancaster to
Poulton services to Hambleton -alight at The Shovels.
Car Parking: Politely in Hambleton
Map: O.S. Pathfinder Sheets 658 Fleetwood & 668
Garstang

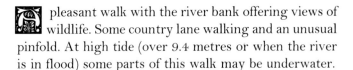 pleasant walk with the river bank offering views of
wildlife. Some country lane walking and an unusual
pinfold. At high tide (over 9.4 metres or when the river
is in flood) some parts of this walk may be underwater.

From The Shovels public house continue along the road
towards Pilling, cross towards the small terrace of shops
by the police station and then turn right in front of
Ryecroft Hall into Carr Lane. Walk the length of this
road and then turn left into Church Lane. Follow this
past the village hall, school and church until it ends at
a T-junction. Turn right onto Ghants Lane, and then
left into Cutts Lane. (1300 metres)

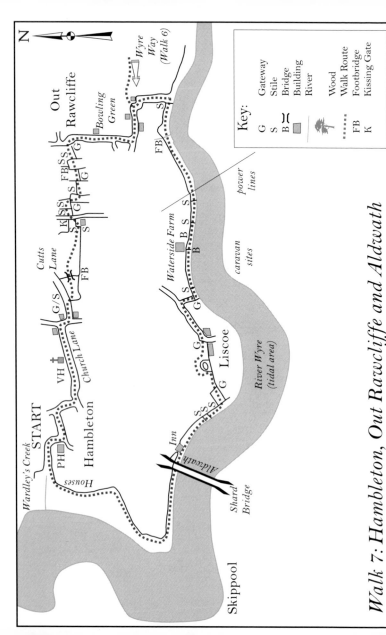

Walk 7: Hambleton, Out Rawcliffe and Aldwath

Go along Cutts Lane but shortly cross the right-hand stile by the gate (with footpath sign) to enter a field to face a cluster of high voltage transmission towers. Go left in the field, pass under more overhead wires, and then walk parallel to the right-hand boundary to go to cross a footbridge in the fence facing you. Cross the next field to a stile in the far right-hand corner, with a modern shed building behind. From the stile a short, but over-grown, enclosed path leads to a further stile and the road. (900 metres)

Cross the road diagonally left to cross a further stile. Follow the right-hand boundary through two fields and then go right through the gate with a stone gatepost in the far right-hand field corner. Walk down the left-hand side of this narrow field but leave it by crossing the stile on your left part way down the field. Go along this field by the left-hand boundary, pass through the gate facing you in the corner and, in the next field, follow near the right-hand boundary to cross a footbridge and stile fac-ing you. Cross the narrow field towards the white house, cross the stile facing you, and then follow near the right-hand field boundary to pass through a gate and reach the road beyond. (700 metres)

Go right along the road to pass the restored pinfold, claimed to be one of only six in Lancashire, and continue, passing the bowling green, through Out Rawcliffe. Ignore a road off to the right to reach a road junction where you go left along Whin Lane, pass a number of houses and, after Quakers Farm, you join the Wyre Way coming in from the left at a right-hand bend in the road. (1300 metres)

Continue down the bending road until it bends left immediately above the river. Leave the road to the right and go over the stile to follow the permissive path along the riverbank. Keep near the right-hand boundary and when you come to cross the footbridge you are back on a public right of way. Keep near the right-hand boundary, with the river to your left, pass under the high voltage lines and, in succession, climb two stiles. After the second stile go slightly away from the right-hand boundary but go to cross a concrete slab bridge and towards the gate in front of Waterside Farm. (1500 metres)

Keep the farm and the boundary to your right and walk along an embankment (the farm access road and a fence to your right). Cross the stile but, shortly after, the way is blocked by a fence. Leave the embankment by going through the gate on your right and then following the enclosed green lane away from the river. At the far end of the track turn left to follow a farm access road (a permissive footpath) up to the front of Liscoe Farm. (1400 metres) The core of the farmhouse is probably an early seventeenth-century construction.

Just beyond the farmhouse the track bends left. The walk goes straight ahead to re-enter the fields by the facing gate. Pass the buildings on your left and then follow the left-hand boundary down the long field, going around the pond in the process. Go through the gate in

The former Shard Toll Bridge

the boundary across your way and in the next field
continue ahead but, just after half way along the boundary, go to cross the stile in the far right-hand corner of
the field and climb the riverside embankment beyond.
(600 metres)

Go right on the embankment, cross the stile and
continue until the way is blocked and there is a stile on
your right. Do not cross this stile but drop down left to
the saltings, then turn right to follow the path along to
pass the Shard Bridge Hotel and arrive at the new Shard
Bridge. (900 metres) On your way you have passed the
site of the old Shard Bridge which itself occupied the
location of an ancient river crossing Aldwath (the old
ford). Whilst we continue along the route of the Wyre
Way we have finished the Garstang to Shard section and

the Wyre Way from here is described in Walk 9.

Continue under the bridge along the edge of the salt-ings to follow the river. The huge sweep of Skippool is best seen when the tide levels permit sailing to take place. After the prominent right-hand gate of Bank Farm go along the embankment top towards the houses at Hambleton. Continue on the shoreward side of the vil-lage to pick up a track that leads you to a road by Wardleys Creek (where the ferry went to Cockle Hall and was the site of another historic harbourage), and, beyond, the hotel. Some of the local boulder clay deposit-s, besides the river, show rocks that came from the Lake District in glaciers. (2500 metres)

On reaching the near side of Wardley's Creek go to the right on the road as it passes a number of houses, bends right and brings us back to the start at The Shovels in Hambleton. (300 metres)

Ordnance Survey Maps: All the maps in this book are hand drawn sketches that are not to scale. They are to give some additional advice to the walker only. The authors believe that it is imperative that you carry and use the relevant Ordnance Survey maps at the 1:25 000 scale. All the walks in this book are covered by four maps. These are Outdoor Leisure series map 41 Forest of Bowland; and three Pathfinder sheets 668 Garstang, 658 Fleetwood and 659 Galgate and Dolphinholme. In the next few years the O.S. will be replacing the Pathfinder series with new maps covering larger areas.

Walk 8

Preesall and Knott End

Preesall – *Wyre Estuary-Knott End – Preesall*
10.5 Km (6 miles) (Wyre Way 3.5 Km)
Start: Centre of Preesall by Saracens Head Public House
(GR 365473)
Bus: Services 88 Lancaster to Fleetwood or 89 Lancaster to
Poulton
Cars: Park politely in Preesall
Map: O.S Pathfinder Sheet 658 Fleetwood

This walk explores the Wyre Estuary and the edge of Morecambe Bay. The route goes through the brine fields and alongside a Site of Special Scientific Interest. The last stages of the Wyre Way (the estuary loop covered in Walk 9) are described from page 61.

From the south side of Preesall's Saracens Head public house go down Back Lane. This lane is followed for some distance until Cemetery Lane goes off to the left. Shortly after, an untidy farmhouse – Corcas – marks where you turn right and go down an enclosed track (marked private road and bridle path), keeping to the right of the brick buildings, to arrive at the small collection of bungalows and caravans at The Heads. (2700 metres)

Walk 8: Preesall and Knott End

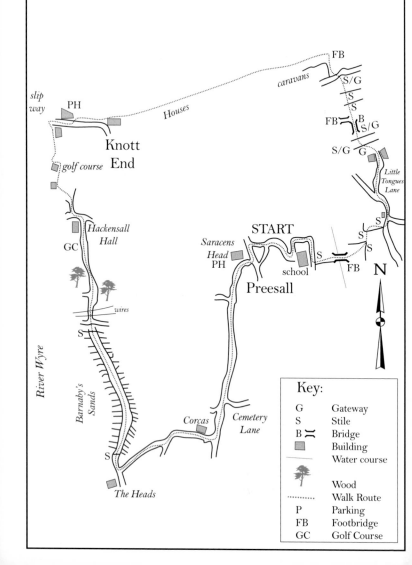

slip way

PH

Houses

caravans

FB

S/G

S

S

B

FB

S/G

S/G

G

Knott End

golf course

Little Tongues Lane

Hackensall Hall

GC

S

S

S

FB

START

Saracens Head PH

school

Preesall

wires

N

River Wyre

S

Barnaby's Sands

Corcas

Cemetery Lane

S

The Heads

Key:

G	Gateway
S	Stile
B ⤫	Bridge
▢	Building
	Water course
🌲	Wood
	Walk Route
P	Parking
FB	Footbridge
GC	Golf Course

❶ *On your way the lane has interesting hedgerows, provides views of the stump of Preesall's windmill and, on more open parts as it meanders amongst the drumlins, views east to the Forest of Bowland and the headwaters of the Wyre.*

(🚶) When you arrive at The Heads the Wyre Way comes along the road from the left. Turn right here, by the Wyre Way signpost and go along the short track to climb the stile and then the embankment beyond. Go straight ahead along the embankment, ignoring paths off to the right, and at the far end cross a stile and arrive at a track by a footpath sign. (1500 metres)

❶ *The saltmarsh to the left is Barnaby's Sands, a Site of Special Scientific Interest (SSSI), managed by the Lancashire Wildlife Trust. This SSSI is an ungrazed saltmarsh, which along with nearby Burrow's Marsh forms a unique wildlife resource in the county. Although the nitrate and phosphate rich waters of the estuary have encouraged the invasion of cord grass (Spartina) since the 1940s, the zonation of vegetation and the occurrence of some flowers such as sea lavender make this a fascinating comparison with grazed saltmarshes. These areas also provide wader and wildfowl roosts and therefore walkers need to minimise any disturbance of roosting birds.*

The area to the right of the embankment is the Preesall saltfield that was re-discovered in 1872 during prospecting for iron ore. The rock salt occurs in 120-metre thick beds and is exceptionally hard – originally it was mined with the help of blasting. The first sample of salt was produced after the prospectors returned to their lodgings and their landlady dissolved, filtered and evaporated the water to produce the mineral.

A mine was opened and salt was taken by a small railway along the track you have now reached to the estuary side where it was shipped out to Australia, South America, the Baltic countries, Canada, India, Burma and Iceland. The few remaining extraction points show where water was used to dissolve the salt and the brine produced pumped out. This left salt pillars between the wells and avoided ground collapse that was once a major problem but created the interesting ponds in the area.

Salt was known in the area earlier, as some of the local names reflect, and there are records from the fifteenth to the eighteenth century of the evaporation of sea water in the locality.

🚶 From the stile go along the track that lies ahead, pass under the two lines of overhead power wires, continue past two small windswept woods, over the lower reaches of the golf course and arrive at the track junction by the side of Hackensall Hall. (1000 metres)

🛈 *The name of the hall is derived from the Viking personal name of Hakon who probably settled in the area in the ninth or early tenth century. The hall was built by Richard and Anne Fleetwood of Rossall in 1656 as their original house site was vulnerable to flooding. There may have been an earlier moated house on the site. During a nineteenth-century renovation it*

Evening sailing, River Wyre

Fleetwood and the Wyre Estuary, from Knott End

is rumoured that two concealed skeletons were found in walls. There are also stories of the house being haunted by a horse. A hoard of around 500 Roman coins was found nearby in 1926.

⊛ Go left at the track junction, bend right through a gateway to keep all the outbuildings to your left, and then turn right to re-enter the golf course by some of their buildings. At the signpost go left and climb across the links to a prominent overhead wire pole by a tin shed. With the estuary and Fleetwood now below you to the left go along the edge of the course and bear left immediately after the garage and cottage to reach the embankment. Go along the embankment to the ferry slipway and the cafés and toilets of Knott End. (1000 metres) You have completed the Wyre Way.

ℹ️ *This is good place to watch the ships and the birds. One story says that the Norse settlers marked the navigable channel of the river by cairns or knotts and the final one being Knott End. The railway, the terminal station now being the café, arrived here in 1908. The ferry to Fleetwood operates seasonally.*

🚶 To continue the walk go along the road away from the slipway and just after the Bourne Arms follow the promenade along the shore of Morecambe Bay. When this ends keep along the shoreward side of the house and the path then follows the protective seawall. After the house the wall passes Brookfield House caravan site and then Sandy Bay caravan site. (1950 metres)

Leave the seawall by the right-hand steps immediately after the caravan site, descend to an enclosed path which is followed, with the caravans on your right, to reach a road. Cross the road diagonally left and re-enter the fields by a stile alongside a gate. Go along the field by the right-hand dyke (Wheal Foot Watercourse). This is followed over two stiles, a footbridge and two stiles besides gates to emerge by another gate onto a track. Bear left on the track and this becomes Little Tongue's Lane as it passes an increasing number of

River Wyre from Knott End (some buildings are now demolished)

houses to reach a larger road by 'Brock' garage. (1500 metres)

Turn left along the road, cross and then continue to a right-hand stile by a bus stop sign on a lamppost just after passing the white bungalow, Pennine View. Over the stile follow the left-hand fence to cross a further stile. Go left to cross the next stile in the fenced field corner and then bear right to cross the footbridge. Climb the steep slope ahead and go over the stile opposite the school grounds. It is worth resting here and looking back at the vista of the Bowland hills and the Fylde plain. Follow the meandering enclosed path to your right and then go down School Lane from the schoolyard to end your walk at the Saracens Head. (750 metres)

Walk 9

The Wyre Estuary Walk

Fleetwood – Stanah – Hambleton – Knott End

25.3 Kilometres (15 miles) – all Wyre Way
Start: Fleetwood Wyre Ferry Terminal (GR 341480)
Bus or Tram: To North Euston Hotel, Fleetwood
(services from Blackpool, Lancaster (via Knott End),
Poulton and Thornton Cleveleys
Cars: Park in Fleetwood near the promenade, or in Knott
End

Map: O.S. Pathfinder Sheet 658 Fleetwood

*The whole of this walk is a loop of the Wyre Way
around the estuary of the river.*

his walk has much to commend it at all times of the
year. In winter during high tide with the waves
rolling against the promenade or, in summer, when the
wildlife can prove interesting. Some sections are impass-
able during very high tides and one section, Skippool to
Shard Bridge, is frequently wet underfoot. On a clear day
you can see three National Parks and three Areas of
Outstanding Natural Beauty.

*The mouth of the Wyre has long been regarded as a sheltered
anchorage and was perhaps the Roman port called Portus*

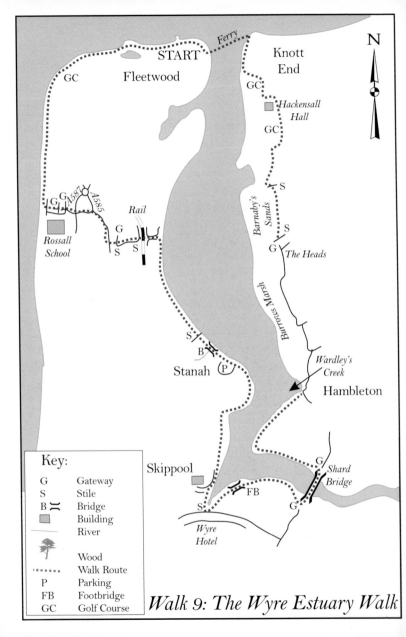

N

Ferry
START
Knott
End
Fleetwood
GC
GC
Hackensall
Hall
GC

G G *A587* *A585*
G
Rail
G
S
Rossall
School
S

S

S
G *The Heads*

Barnaby's
Sands

Burrows Marsh

S
B)(
Stanah
P

Wardley's
Creek

Hambleton

Skippool

FB
G *Shard*
Bridge

S
G

Wyre
Hotel

Key:

G	Gateway
S	Stile
B)(	Bridge
▪	Building
	River
🌳	Wood
•••••	Walk Route
P	Parking
FB	Footbridge
GC	Golf Course

Walk 9: The Wyre Estuary Walk

Setantiorum. The mouth of the estuary is actually narrower than much of the estuary and, in much earlier geological times, the river may have reached the sea nearer Blackpool. This walk is a fine and fitting conclusion to a river that the Wyre Way has followed from source to sea.

From the ferry slipway, opposite the North Euston turn right to pass the RNLI lifeboat station and shop, the small lighthouse and then arrive at the diminutive pier. Just beyond the pier turn right to follow the track to the sea edge promenade. From here follow the roadway and then concrete sea defence wall all the way past the marine lake, around Rossall Point, past the golf course (where the route is paralleled by a bridleway to the shore side of the sea wall) and continue heading south towards Blackpool Tower. Eventually the high left-hand wall becomes lower by a gate and lifebuoy and with the number G23 attached. Go left through the gap to leave the sea defence. (4800 metres)

From the gap go down the ramp and through the gate. Follow the right-hand fence down the field, with Rossall School beyond. These fields have

Pharos Lighthouse, Fleetwood

been allocated for housing development. After the small second field go through a further gate to follow the school access road round to the right and then left to meet the main A587 road. Cross the road and tram track carefully and go down the facing Rossall Lane (B5409) to reach the main Amounderness Way (A585). Cross this directly to go along a further lane that is followed to its far end where it joins a road opposite a caravan site. (1800 metres)

❶ *The name Rossall is thought to be derived from the Celtic Rhos meaning moor. The Abbey of Dieulacres in Staffordshire once owned the land around the school but on dissolution it came into the hands of the Fleetwood and Fleetwood-Hesketh family. The land was given to the school in 1844 and once contained Rossall Hall of which little now remains.*

🚶 Go right down this next road but cross over to the left-hand pavement. Walk along to the end of the caravan site and immediately after a short terrace of houses turn left. With the industrial buildings on your right go towards a gate way but cross the stile and follow along the raised bank-top path with old hawthorns forming an avenue. At the end of the bank cross the stile and the railway line. Go forward through a gap between the high metal fences and the enclosed path leads you to the river bank. (1500 metres)

❶ *The huge former industrial complex was originally the*

Fleetwood Salt Company that processed rock salt and brine from the salt field across the Wyre and which the route will later cross. The brine was pumped under the river. The plant eventually came into the ownership of ICI but is now a shadow of its former industrial self.

🚶 Turn right alongside the site fence with the estuary to your left. When the track forks go left (where the pipes go under the track) and continue along the right-hand fence to a stile. Over the stile the path is above a caravan site to your right and eventually leads, by a bridge over a feeder dyke to the Wyre, to a car park and the Wyre Ecology centre and Stanah Country Park. (2400 metres)

ℹ️ *This area, now in the creative care of Wyre Borough Council,*

Wyre Estuary, Skippool

has a car park, picnic site and visitor centre by the estuary. In the 1960s the saltmarsh was enclosed by embankment and used as a council refuse tip (would we let such civic vandalism happen today?) but was reclaimed in the 1980s. The centre has an information point, exhibitions of the estuary's wildlife and heritage, small shop, refreshments and toilets.

To continue the walk go left (from where you met the road) on the road, go under the barrier and then take the path off to the left and down to the edge of the salt marsh. From here to Skippool, Shard Bridge and on to Wardleys the path may be affected by very high tides. The surfaced path, (signed Cockle Hall and Skippool), clings to the side of the estuary as it passes the Cockle Hall picnic site (see the information board), goes round

Wyre Estuary, Skippool

the bay called Ramper Pool, and then bends to pass a plethora of moored boats with their precarious timber walkways to reach the sailing club base. Go in front of the sailing club base, continue along the track and the road which follows the river, then Skippool Creek and a side creek before bending right again to pass a hotel (Thornton Lodge). Leave the road by the footpath sign to the left and follow the creek-side path towards a stile that, if climbed, would access the road almost opposite the tall River Wyre pub. (3300 metres)

Do not cross the stile but go left over the culverted creek and then left again in the field with the creek again on your left. Follow the left-hand edge towards a footpath sign, cross the bridge, climb the short surfaced footpath and again follow the left-hand edge of the field towards the River Wyre. Bear right above the river, follow the field edge along to the far left-hand corner where some steps descend to a boardwalk. Descend the steps and follow the frequently wet path near the right-hand edge of the salt marsh towards Shard Bridge. A track leads up the embankment to a gate to reach the road over the bridge. Go left over the bridge to the far bank. (2000 metres)

❶ *Edward III noted Skippool in 1330 when he granted a road from Poulton. The pool, through Main Dyke, drains Blackpool's important nature reserve, Marton Mere. Skippool was a harbour in the sixteenth and seventeenth centuries when wines, spirits, tea, tobacco, rum, sugar and timber were*

Wyre Estuary, Skippool

imported. The Shard Bridge was built in the 1990s to replace the toll bridge of 1864. The site is Aldwath, one of the old fords of the Wyre – the name deriving from the Norse.

At the end of the bridge turn left and go past the gate down to the salt marsh. Go right, along the edge of the saltings to follow the river. By the prominent gate of Bank Farm go along the embankment top towards the houses at Hambleton. Continue on the shoreward side of the village to pick up a track that leads you to a road. Turn left to reach Wardleys Creek (where the ferry went to Cockle Hall and was the site of another historic harbourage) and the hotel. Some of the local boulder clay deposits beside the river show rocks that came from the Lake District in glaciers. (2500 metres)

From here to The Heads the Wyre Way continues along narrow lanes, keeping left at any junctions, passing the hamlet of Staynall and Burrows Marsh (a Site of Special Scientific Interest). (3500 metres)

From The Heads to Knott End the route is described in Walk 8. (3500 metres)

Woodlands: Lancashire has a very low percentage cover of woodlands and the Forestry Commission regards the county as suitable for much more planting. Some of this future planting may be of conifers or of native woodland trees. Many of the walks in this book rely on woodlands for adding variety to the landscape and anyone who doesn't know the county and has only used these walks could be forgiven for thinking that the county is well wooded.

Despite the plethora of woodlands seen from these walks here are a few thoughts that may put them more in context. In the Fylde area the flat landscape looks well wooded due to the number of hedgerow trees that are seen. However, many of these are old and not being replaced. In the Bowland foothills there is a mixture of woodlands. Some are maintained for pheasant rearing or form part of a rough shoot. Other rectangular block woodlands of conifers look strangely placed in a rounded landscape. The more deciduous woodlands, for example along the Brock, look at their best in autumn but many are poorly managed.

Sycamore and beech are common in the area yet these attractive trees are often growing at the expense of native species and so can be detrimental to wildlife. There is a case for restoring more of these woodlands as native woodlands that will have a more representative ground flora (see the bluebells during spring to see what we might be missing).

Walk 10

Mills on the Calder

Garstang – Calder Vale – Garstang

8 kilometres (5 miles)

Start: Garstang Discovery Centre (GR 493454)

Bus: Grastang lies on the main Preston to Lancaster route (services 40, 41) and Lancaster to Blackpool route (services 42 and X42)

Cars: Park by Garstang Discovery Centre

O.S. Map: Outdoor Leisure Sheet 41 – Forest of Bowland

---

walk mostly over field paths and tracks that combines aspects of industrial archaeology with fine prospects of the landscape. In bluebell time the woods along the route can be spectacular, but this walk is an all year round favourite because of the views across the Fylde plain to the coast.

From the Discovery Centre go across the car park to the river and follow the paved path upstream, with the sports field on your left, to reach the embankment and bridge across the River Wyre. Go up the steps on the left near-side and go over the bridge and continue to the stile facing you beyond the tarmac track. (400 metres)

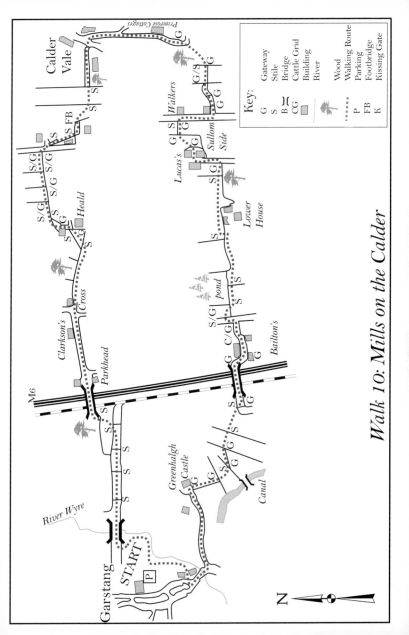

Walk 10: Mills on the Calder

The Lancaster Canal at Garstang

ⓘ *The bridge was formerly the crossing point of the old Garstang to Knott End railway known locally as the 'Pilling Pig'. It operated, largely unsuccessfully, between 1870 and 1963.*

⊛ Continue along the enclosed path, the former line of the railway, down over a small stream, up to cross a stile and along to cross the next stile under the overhead power lines. Continue along but as the trackbed goes into a cutting follow up the left-hand embankment to a stile by a seat. (600 metres)

ⓘ *The cutting took the railway to join the mainline at the former Garstang and Catterall Station but now forms a memorial* *nature reserve to which you have permissive access. In the cutting are smaller exposures of the underlying friable sandstone, a rock that serves as an aquifer.*

(🚶) Over the stile go half right across the field, pass the corner of the wood and climb the tall stile by the gate in the far corner of the field. Turn right on the track to cross over the railway and, along with a stream, the motorway to reach Parkhead. (300 metres)

Go straight up the metalled access track, passing Clarkson's Farm on your left, and up to meet the road where it bends. Your way is directly across to the right of Cross Cottage and you walk up the track towards Heald Farm. (500 metres) The house is named after the site of a wailing cross, whose base stone is apparently now buried, where coffin bearers could rest and the mourners wail.

Just short of the buildings of Heald Farm turn left over a stile into the bottom of the second wood after Cross Cottage. Go up the 'open' wood, near the left-hand fence, and leave it by the stile and gate in the top corner. Go left along the short track to cross a stile by a gate and corrugated iron barn and then go ahead into the field by another gateway by a ladder stile. Turn right and follow the right-hand boundary up to the top of the field. (600 metres)

(ℹ️) *This is the highest point of the walk and from where extensive views across the Fylde to the coast and the Lake District can be seen. Eastward lies the moors of the Forest of Bowland AONB.*

(X) Go through the gap stile by the gate and continue down by the right-hand boundary through two further gap stiles by gates (part of the boundary is a line of beech trees) to reach the road by a further stile and gate. Turn right and cross the road diagonally towards the gateway to 'The Paddock' and, in front of the gate, go right along a short enclosed path and cross the stile at the end. Continue by the right-hand ditch and, over the stile in the corner, go left along a short enclosed path to cross a short footbridge and re-enter the fields. Go diagonally right to cross a stile to the right of the electricity pole and then cross the narrow field to an obvious stile by the corner of the wood. (550 metres)

From here an enclosed path leads past the wood, some rear gardens and down some steps to the road into Calder Vale. (200 metres) The centre of the village and the last working mill are down to the left.

(i) *Calder Vale is a most unexpected site – an industrial stone-built village enveloped in the fold of the Bowland hills. The vernacular architecture is not without character. The mill was built as a four-storey cotton mill in 1835 with thick stone outer walls and cast-iron pillars. There are remains of the former mill-race and mill-pond above the village. The waterwheel was replaced by a turbine, later, by a beam engine and in 1909 a gas engine, but is now electrically driven. The mill and village were built for the Jacksons, a Quaker family. The lack of a public house in the village is due to the family not wishing to see 'ragged children'. Brothers Richard and Jonathan founded the cotton mill whilst brother John opened a paper mill upstream at Oakenclough.*

🚶 From where you emerged on the road turn right down Albert Terrace and follow along the track to the isolated terrace of Primrose Cottages. (450 metres)

ⓘ *The track goes through steep-sided woodlands that are carpeted in bluebells each May, passes above the lodge of the other village mill and the rocky-bed of the River Calder to reach the terrace formerly comprising twelve mill workers cottages and the mill-owner's house. The Barnacre Weaving Mill has been demolished but reservoir sites and a mill-race can be seen from our route. This mill, sited beyond the cottages, opened in 1845 and was powered originally by a waterwheel and later by a steam engine whose chimney was constructed up the hillside.*

🚶 Continue past the cottages and gate until the track bends left. Go right and climb the sloping path up through the wood to re-enter the open fields by a gate. Follow the left-hand fence to cross a stile by a gate in the far left-hand field corner and then continue ahead and down, by two further gates, to reach the road by Sullom Side Farm. (650 metres)

Follow the road to the right to reach the next building, Walker House. Cross the road to re-enter the fields by a gate and stile. Go down the first field by the right-hand boundary, pass through a gate, and go diagonally left to eventually enter the rear of Lucas's Farm by a gate. (550 metres)

Go down the right-hand side of the house, turn left on the farm access road and, after twenty metres, go through a small field gate on your right just prior to a small wood. Go down the wood edge, over a further stile and go down the field to cross a stile in the far left-hand corner (beyond the outbuildings of the huge rebuilt Lower House). (250 metres)

Cross this stile, turn right, and go to a stile in the far right-hand corner of the field that lies opposite a pond in Janet's Hill Wood – a wood with a eucalyptus tree planted in the 1990s as a memorial to a soldier who died in Burma in 1945. Continue along the right-hand boundary to the corner of the wood (the tree is to your right), cross the stile and go left across the field to cross a further stile by a gate some 20 metres from the left-hand corner. (300 metres)

Cross the road and, over the cattle grid, go down the access track to Bailton's Farm. Continue down and right through the gated, cobbled yard to cross the bridges over both the motorway and the railway line. (500 metres)

From this last bridge go down the track and, where the hedge on your right ends by a gate, squeeze through the gap stile. Cross the next field towards the right of a lone oak tree standing proud of the far boundary where you will find

Greenhalgh (Garstang) Castle

a further stile to cross. Directly cross the short field, aiming left of the pylon, to pass through a gate and then follow the left-hand boundary to the field corner where you cross the stile and plank footbridge facing you. (400 metres)

[If, instead, you want to return to Garstang by the canal towpath you can access it by going through the adjacent gate in the field corner and walking a short distance to a canal bridge and steps. (1500m)]

Cross the next field, parallel to the canal, aiming to the left of the farm buildings ahead. At the fence/hedge junction go directly ahead through the gateway and follow the left-hand hedge along to reach the yard, by a gate, of Greenhalgh Castle Farm. (400 metres)

❶ *The farm is a seventeenth-century building with stone mullion windows. The stone was 'quarried' from the castle that was built to guard the ford over the Wyre in 1490 by the first earl of Derby. This was one of the last strongholds in Lancashire to hold out against parliament in the Civil War.*

(🚶) Go left along the farm access road to reach the road bridge over the Wyre. Turn right along the road and then go right along the riverside path back to the start of the walk. (1000 metres)

> **River Wyre:** the name of the river gives the name to the local district council. The name is possibly a Celtic derivative of the Welsh 'Gwyar' meaning blood water, a possible description of the reddish-brown peat load carried by the river in spate. The river rises in the Bowland fells above Abbeystead before flowing 26 miles to the sea at Fleetwood and Knott End.

Walk 11

Amongst Pheasants –
Exploring Barnacre

Garstang – Barnacre or Lady Hamilton's Well –
Garstang

8.9 kilometres (5.4 miles) (shorter route 6.3 Kilometres, 4
miles)
Start: Garstang Discovery Centre (GR 493454)
Bus: Garstang lies on the main Preston to Lancaster route
(services 40, 41) and Lancaster to Blackpool Route
(services 42 and X42)
Cars: Parking by the Garstang Discovery Centre
Map: O.S. Outdoor Leisure 41 Forest of Bowland

walk along field paths and a return along the canal.
The full walk and the shorter option both have
elevated viewpoints worthy of the minor efforts of the
walk. The former Barnacre Estate is an area where
pheasants can always be seen crossing your path and
sometimes the quiet walkers will see the more secretive
roe deer.

From the Discovery Centre go through the rear car
park to the river and follow it along the sports field
edge path along the river and climb the steps up the

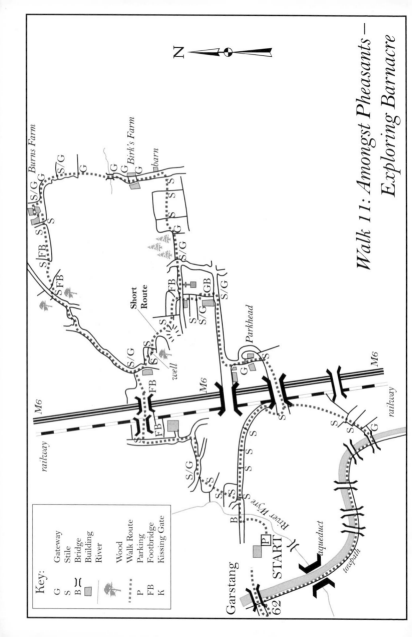

Walk 11: Amongst Pheasants – Exploring Barnacre

Key:
- G — Gateway
- S — Stile
- B — Bridge
- ☐ — Building
- 🌲 — Wood
- ⋯ — Walk Route
- P — Parking
- FB — Footbridge
- K — Kissing Gate

Barns Farm

Birk's Farm

barn

Short Route

well

Parkhead

M6

railway

railway

M6

M6

River Wyre

aqueduct

towpath

Garstang

START

62

near side of the bridge abutment. (370 metres) The bridge crosses the extraction point from the Lune–Wyre Conjunctive Use Scheme and from here it is piped to the Frank Law Treatment works at Catterall before joining the North West supply grid. The upstream barriers are to prevent flood waters from inundating villages down stream.

Go over the bridge and just after the embankment track has joined from the left go down to cross a stile and then across the field to a further stile. In the next field continue in the same direction to cross a further stile near the right-hand field corner. Go across the next field to the left-hand boundary, which is followed to a stile by a gate, and access to Wyre Lane. (500 metres)

Go right along the lane, bear left at the junction and continue up to meet the metalled road where you turn left. Follow this until the end of the field after the farm entrance track on your right. Go over the

stiled footbridge to enter the field and follow the left-hand hedge along. Cross the railway footbridge and the following bridge over the motorway. Continue directly up the field to cross a stile by a gate in the top left-hand field corner. Here you have the choice of two routes. See p.91 for lady Hamilton's Well and a shorter route. (1100 metres)

The main route goes left along the road, ignores the road off to the left and climbs to a further road junction. Keep left here, continue uphill on the road, pass the wood on your right, and then opposite the wood on your left go to cross a stile on your right. Leave this first field by the footbridge just to your left and then bear half right, aiming to the right of Burns Farm, to cross the next stiled footbridge. Follow the right-hand boundary up to the farm, cross the two consecutive stiles facing you and then go forward and then left to enter the farmyard. Burns Farm is sometimes open for refreshments but check in advance. (1300 metres)

Turn right to leave the farmyard, then go right on the track. This bends almost immediately to the left to a stile and gate. Beyond these continue uphill along the track, pass through a further gate and then continue on this track near the right-hand fence towards a stile and gate in the far right-hand corner of the field. Cross the stile and follow the right-hand fence along to pass through a small gate in the far right-hand field corner. Cross the next field by aiming for the buildings of Birks Farm and, at the far side of the field, go down to a gate and stream.

Climb towards the farm on the track beyond the gate, go through the gated farmyard and leave by following along the farm access road to reach a field barn with a red pantiled roof on your left. (800 metres)

Go further along the access road but look for a stile on your right where the hedge has a fenced gap. Cross this double stile and go ahead to cross a further stile in the field boundary across your way. In the next field go down by the remains of a right-hand ditch and former hedge line to cross a stile in the fence across your way. Go down again towards the left-hand corner of the wood ahead, go through the wood side gate and follow the right-hand boundary of the wood down the field to reach the road by a gate and a double stile. Take the road directly ahead to reach Barnacre Church and the shorter route described below. (1100 metres)

❶ *Barnacre Church has interesting stained glass windows depicting saints and, if open, is worth looking inside. Along with Scorton Church (Walk 4) it was designed by Paley and Austin.*

🚶 From the road outside the lower church gate go left up a few steep stone steps to follow a short enclosed path between the churchyard and the vicarage. Cross the stile at the end, follow the left-hand fence along to cross a further stile by a gate and continue through a further gate along a track besides the right-hand farm buildings. Cross a stile and a narrow bridge to your left, turn right and leave the field by a stile to the right of the gate near the right-hand field corner. (250 metres)

(🚶) Go right down the metalled Parkhead Lane until a track goes left by a garage. Turn left here and follow the track along, through the yard of the former farmstead and emerge to climb a stile into the field beyond. A bypass route, to the left of the farm, has been provided – a further case of new non-agricultural owners not liking historic rights of way through their property. Over the stile go right and down to cross the motorway and railway bridge. A second railway bridge over the disused Pilling Pig line then follows. (500 metres)

(ℹ️) *A short route to Garstang can be taken from the stile to the near right-hand side of this bridge, going steeply left down to the old track-bed, through the permissive path in the 'Wildgoose Reserve' and then straight along to Garstang.*

(🚶) Go ahead over this second bridge and enter the field by a stile. Turn left in the field but begin to bear right away from the left-hand fence to cross the middle of the field where there is a small change of field level that marks the line of a former hedgerow. (A pylon also gives a general guide to your direction over the field.) At the far side of the field go to cross the stile in the bent field corner just beyond a footpath sign. In the next field follow the right-hand hedge to cross a stile in the far right-hand corner. Continue ahead, through the gate,

Lancaster Canal, near Castle Farm

and along the track to the bridge over the canal. (700 metres)

Go down the steps on the right of the bridge and descend to the canal towpath. With the canal on your right go along to Garstang. The road bridge after the aqueduct is where you leave and cross the canal and go through the town back to your starting point. (2250 metres)

The shorter route via Lady Hamilton's Well

For the shorter route indicated on p.88, go right along the road until you are opposite Slack House Farm. Turn left, through a gate, to go down a short enclosed track

Canal Boats at Garstang

and then cross the stile on the right just after the stream.
Cross the damp field aiming for the clump of sycamore,
holly and alder trees in the left-hand corner. (300 metres)
In this clump lie the remains of Lady Hamilton's Well.

ⓘ *Hewitson describes this as 'The Spa Well' where the Hamilton
family used to bathe when they stayed at Woodacre Hall (no
longer standing). Lady Hamilton moved into the area after
the death of her husband and perhaps it was her use of this
spring-fed well, with its alleged medicinal properties that has
led to its current name.*

ⓧ Go to cross the stile in the left-hand corner of the field
by the wood, and then climb the steep bank with the

wood on your right. At the top there are extensive views of Morecambe Bay and the Lakeland fells. From the top of the slope head to the right of the stone-built house, pass the vegetated and rabbit infested depression of 'Delph Quarry' down to your right, and go to cross a stile, in the fence, which is a continuation of a stone wall, in the far left-hand corner of the field. Go down by the right-hand fence until you reach a footbridge that enables you to cross the stream and climb the steps to the road outside Barnacre Church. (300 metres) From here rejoin the main walk at page 89.

Walk 12

Fellside Parish and Ancient People

Calder Vale – Bleasdale – Calder Vale

14 km (9 miles)
Start: Calder Vale (GR 533458)
Bus: 212 Brookhouse to Garstang (restricted service)
Car Parking: Park politely in the village.

Map: O.S. Leisure Series Sheet 41 Forest of Bowland

This walk combines the best of footpaths near the River Calder as well as a section along the River Brock. It meanders through woodlands yet provides excellent views of the fells and the Fylde plain. The site of a prehistoric 'woodhenge' is also visited. Walkers who want a longer ramble can start at Garstang and combine this route with Walk 10 to provide a 24 km (15 mile) circuit. Whilst some paths are often wet there are also plenty of dry-shod kilometres on footpaths over private estate roads and tracks.

Start from the bridge over the River Calder below the shop and go left, with the mill and church to your right, to follow the road along Long Row cottages but carry straight on on the sign-posted path (to the church) where the road swings right behind the cottages. The

Walk 12: Fellside Parish and Ancient People

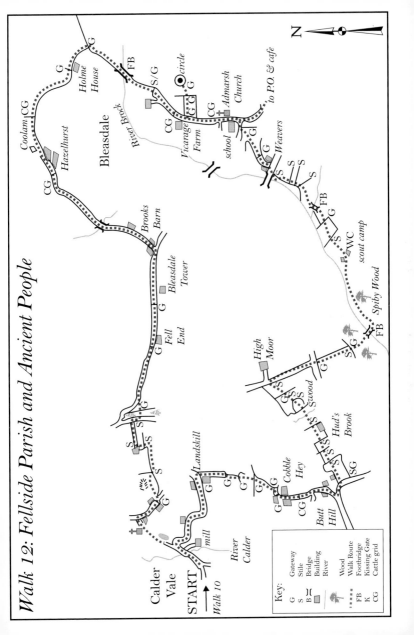

N

Holme House

G

G

Coolam CG

Hazelhurst

CG

G

Bleasdale

River Brook

FB

S/G

circle

G
G
Vicarage CG
Farm
CG

CG
G
Admarsh
Church

to P.O. & café

school
G

G
Weavers

S

S
S
S
S

G

FB

G

WC
scout camp

Brooks
Barn

Bleasdale
Tower

G

Fell
End

G

S

S

Spiby Wood

FB
S/G

High
Moor

G
G
S

S
S

S wood

S
S
Hud's
Brook
S

SG

Landskill

G
G
G
G
G

Cobble
Hey
G
G
CG

Butt
Hill

G

mill

Calder
Vale

START

Walk 10

River
Calder

Key:

G   Gateway
S   Stile
B   )(Bridge
     Building
     River
.... Walk Route
FB Footbridge
K   Kissing Gate
CG Cattle grid

G   Gateway
S   Stile
B   Bridge
     Wood
.... Walk Route
FB Footbridge
K
CG

tarmacadamed path leads past the mill lodge, alongside the river and then climbs through the wood to the church and school beyond. (800 metres)

Continue ahead to the road junction and go right (even though sign-posted back to Calder Vale), pass Lower Landskill farm and yard and then go through the gate beyond the last building. Turn left up the field, keeping a fenced old quarry to your left, and climb a wall stile in the top right-hand corner of the field where the wall meets the fence. (500 metres)

Follow the left-hand fence and streamlet up, turn left when the fence bends left to cross a stile and then aim for a stile to the right of Rough Moor house. Walk right up the access drive and then right along the road. After the bend in the road go through a gap stile in the wall on your left (signposted) and after a short depth of trees emerge through a small gate into the field and up to the access track ahead. (500 metres)

ⓘ *During your climb from Calder Vale the views were back across the Fylde plain to the coast. Now it is towards the fells that off-shoot from the Pennine chain – the hills of the Forest of Bowland, Longridge Fell, Beacon Fell and, to the south, the heights around Winter Hill.*

🚶 Turn right along the metalled estate road, pass through the gate by Fell End Farm and, after a further gate go by the rear of Bleasdale Tower that was built as a shooting lodge in the mid-nineteenth century. Continue down the road to the junction, and post box, at Brook's Barn Farm. (1550 metres)

Go left by the farmhouse and follow the track along passing stone buildings on the right, over a bridge and up through a wood, across a field and arrive at a cattle grid to the right-hand side of Hazelhurst Farm. (1250 metres)

ⓘ *The first buildings passed were once a reformatory school but the boys from urban backgrounds were extensively used as 'inexpensive' estate workers. The bridge you cross (with a date plaque on one face and a mason's stone on the right parapet) was part of their work. They used to turn the fields*

Fairsnape Fell and Bleasdale

by hand. Hazelhurst and the adjacent Coolam (near the ruined cottage you soon pass on your left) were once local wool-producing villages inhabited by around 70 people. Most of these were involved in wool spinning and handloom weaving prior to the goods being sent by packhorse to the wool towns of East Lancashire and Yorkshire.

Continue along the track just below the fellside and pass over a cattle grid and continue down the track to reach the rear of Holme House Farm. Go through the gate ahead, through the yard and then through a further gate before following a farm track along and over a bridge. This grassy track continues by a right-hand wall where is becomes a 'concessionary' path, crosses a stream and

Fiendsdale Head, Bleasdale

then follows a left-hand fence to a gate and stile. Over the stile go ahead to pick up the estate road with Admarsh farm down to your right. Go directly along this road to cross a cattle grid and then, on the right, the access to Vicarage Farm. (1750 metres)

ⓘ *Opposite the entrance to Vicarage Farm is a kissing gate and a gate to your left. This gives access to Bleasdale Circle. To reach the circle site cross this field up to a further kissing gate in the top left-hand corner and then cross to a further kissing gate in the clump of trees that hide the circle site. Return by this route to the estate road. (750 metres) The circle site is marked now by unsightly concrete stumps where once eleven wooden posts stood. In the central area was a small barrow whose excavation yielded graves with two cremations in collared urns and an incense cup. A ditch and a timber palisade surrounded the 50-metre circle. This unique woodhenge site has been dated at various times but the on-site information suggests around 1700 BC. The entrance to the circle points towards the Fairsnape ridge where lies the man-made gouge into the ridge called 'Nicks Chair'. Was it a contemporary alignment with the circle?*

⚐ From Vicarage Farm continue along the estate road to reach Admarsh Church and then continue down to the village hall (on the left) and school (right) just beyond which is a road junction. This is a nineteenth-century church building with a 'quaint' Last Supper over the altar and two odd faces peering from carvings on old chairs. It is the only known dedication to St Eadnor who was possibly, the Eadbert who carried on St Cuthbert's work at Lindisfarne and was buried in the saint's tomb. (750 metres)

If you are in need of refreshment continue the 750 metres directly ahead to Bleasdale Post Office but then retrace your steps to the school.

Just after the school turn right and follow this metalled estate road with beech hedges on each side until you reach the first gate with stone gate posts on your left. Go through the gate to enter the field and go diagonally right to cross to a fence corner and continue in the same direction with the fence on your right. This leads to a gate and then, via a short enclosed track, through the gated yard of Weaver's Farm and on to the road. (750 metres)

Cross the road diagonally right, and climb the bank to cross a stile to enter the wood. Follow along the left-hand boundary fence and after 200 metres cross a stile over to your left to go into the field. Turn right and go down the field by the right-hand fence to the wood, over two further stiles, to cross a stile by the far corner of the wood. (Some people continue in the wood all the way to this corner but the above description is the line of the right of way.) The path now descends steeply near the right-hand fence, crosses a small field to reach a foot-bridge – Jack Anderton's Bridge – over the left-hand branch of the River Brock. (550 metres)

Walk downstream by the right-hand fence, pass through a gate and then continue over one of two adjacent stiles to enter the grounds of Wood Top Scout Camp. Follow along the wide path until the path reaches the near-side of the camp toilet block. (550 metres)

The actual rights of way through here and the next woodland are somewhat complex and often very wet. One route, sometimes well used, is to veer right at the toilet block and follow tracks as near as possible to the river on your right. There are some wet patches and some greasy and narrow bits of path as you enter Spiby, formerly the more appropriately-named Boggy Wood. This was a favourite spot of the late Cyril Spiby, a Preston Rambler and guidebook writer. The path emerges at a footbridge adjacent to where the rough Snape Rake Lane (possibly the route of the Roman Road from Ribchester to Lancaster) fords the river. (750 metres)

Cross the footbridge and climb Snape Rake up to cross a stile by a gate, and then follow the leveller track through an avenue of trees to reach a road junction. (500 metres)

Follow the Oakenclough road (Delph Lane) straight ahead and after about 600 metres) cross a stone step stile in the left-hand wall diagonally opposite the entrance drive to High Moor Farm. Cross the field diagonally left to cross the fence by a ladder stile by a gate and then the next field towards the enclosed wood. You enter the wood by a stone step stile to the right of the mid point, follow the path directly across the Huds Brook Wood and then re-enter the fields by a further stone step stile. (1250 metres)

Cross the field to a farm bridge over a small ditch and then aim 20 metres above the farm buildings to cross a stile with a tall marker post. Cross the middle of the next field by keeping parallel to the left-hand wall to cross a further stile. Continue parallel to the right-hand fence until two adjacent stiles can be seen ahead. Over these climb the slight rise and then bear slightly right to cross another pair of stiles. Descend the next field beside the right-hand boundary to reach a road by a stile adjacent to the gate in the far right-hand corner. (650 metres)

Turn right along the road but almost immediately turn right again along the access track to Butt Hill Farm. Keep to the left of the main buildings, pass Infield house and Sullom View to your left and continue over the cattle grid to reach the cobbled yard of Cobble Hey Farm. (1000 metres)

A gate on your right just after the farmhouse enables you to follow a track by the righthand wall and pass through a further gate. Continue near the right-hand wall but as this begins to bend away to the right go ahead and down the field to a gate in the hollow where a wall and fence meet. Go through this gate (and its stream) and turn right to follow the track by the right-hand fence up to pass through a further gate. In the next field follow the right-hand fence as it bends round and leads you to pass through a further gate beyond which an enclosed track leads to Landskill farms. (800 metres)

Turn left after the first farmhouse and go down through the gate, past the elegant front of the vernacular Jacobean farmhouse where once Catholics held forbidden services. The farm access road goes down a lane, bears right through a field and then left by some buildings. It leads down to Long Row and to the centre of Calder Vale. (750 metres)

The Forest of Bowland: received its name not from woodland cover but because it was covered by laws applying to its status as a royal forest. These game preserves were set up largely after the Norman Conquest. The forest law could be harsh on local residents, especially if they had been poaching. This part of Lancashire had a number of hunting forests. The upper reaches of the Wyre were, for example, part of the Royal Forest of Wyresdale.

Walk 13

The Badger's River

Brock – Bleasdale – Claughton – Brock

20 Kilometres (12 miles) – with a shorter alternative
Start: A6 Road at Brock by Dutton Forshaw Garage (GR
512406)
Bus: Service 40 & 41 Lancaster – Garstang – Preston
Service to Brock Green Man (now Brock Tavern)
Cars: At Brock Tavern (Formerly the Green Man) 01995
640220

Map: O.S. Outdoor Leisure Sheet 41 Forest Of Bowland

The middle and upper reaches of the River Brock are a long-time favourite area for Lancashire ramblers. Much of the river can be followed close to its banks, there is delightful scenery and good opportunities for seeing river birds such as the dipper, pied and yellow wagtail or kingfisher. The higher fields are the haunt of curlews and sandpipers whilst pheasants are abundant. Many of the paths can be very muddy, as are many of the fields on the return route. Some stiles on the return paths are more like mini hurdles but the walk is excellent especially in autumn when the riverside woodlands are at their best.

Walk 13: The Badger's River

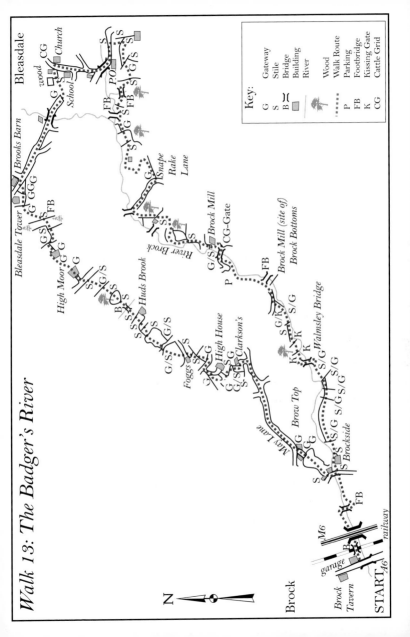

N

Bleasdale

Brock

Brock Tavern

START

M6

A6 railway

garage

Brook Barn

Bleasdale Tower

High Moor

Wood

Church

School

P.O.

CG

Snape Rake Lane

River Brock

Brock Mill

Brock Mill (site of)

Brock Bottoms

Huds Brook

High House

Clarkson's

Foggs

Brow Top

Walmsley Bridge

Brockside

May Lane

Key:

G	Gateway
S	Stile
B)(	Bridge
▢	Building
~	River
⋯	Walk Route
🌲	Wood
P	Parking
FB	Footbridge
K	Kissing Gate
CG	Cattle Grid

(🚶) The path starts immediately adjacent to the building of the Land Rover garage and goes through their outdoor display to a bridge over the railway line at the site of the former Brock station. Follow the track ahead and go under the M6 and continue with the river on your right until you can cross it by an aluminium footbridge. Continue along the access road on the far bank to reach New Bridge. (1300 metres)

Cross the road directly and pass through a gap stile and follow the enclosed path by the riverbank until it comes to a stile at the end of the buildings. (Once rural fields and a farm, Brock Side is now a suburbanised housing development.) From the stile cross the mown area and cross the next stile by the gate. In the field follow the long left-hand fence above the river and leave it by the stile and gate at the far end (note the small waterfall in the Brock). Continue by the left-hand hedge, cross another stile by a gate, go along a short enclosed track and cross a further stile by a gate. In the next field keep below the line of trees to reach Walmsley Bridge by a stile by a gate. (1300 metres)

Go left over Walmsley Bridge, noting its dates, and immediately re-enter a field by the kissing gate on your right. Cross the field to avoid the meander of the river and then pass through a short wood with kissing gates at each end. Cross the next field keeping near the left-hand fence but as the field narrows go over the stile near the river. Follow the riverbank path along, cross the stile and gate of a temporary enclosure, again at a narrowing

106

of the field, and continue near the bank until an old hedge-bank comes down towards you. Go over the foot-bridge to the left of this hedge and follow the hedge up to pass through a kissing gate by a gate to reach a track. (1100 metres)

Go right down the track, pass the remains of the site of Brock Corn Mill – later making files for metalworkers – continuing along a path with the river near to your right-hand for some distance. You pass through open spaces and woodlands and eventually emerge on the road at Brock Mill by Higher Brock Bridge adjacent to the picnic site and car park. (1400 metres)

Go over the bridge and immediately turn left to pass through the gap stile by the gateway. Keep left below Brock Mill and the adjacent house and then climb the

By Waddecar Scout Camp

stile by the gate. Go by the right-hand fence and then turn right as it bends right. When it bends again continue directly ahead to pick up the left-hand fence adjacent to the river. Follow this fence along and cross the stile in the far left-hand corner of the field. The path now continues between the river and the right-hand fence until, at the end of the right-hand field, it bends away from the river, climbs through a narrow wood and the bluff beyond to reach a track. Go left down the track and just before the former cottage, with the aqueduct to your left, leave the track to enter the edge of the wood. The path now follows the fence line at the bottom of the wood, with a field to your left, to again reach the river bank. Follow this along to meet the footbridge over the Brock and where Snape Rake Lane crosses the river. (1300 metres) A shorter route can be taken by crossing the river, as described in walk 12, and rejoining our route near Huds Brook.

Go right and up the sunken hollow of Snape Rake Lane. Continue along it when it becomes tarred, cross its highest point, and as it bends right the wood on your left gives way to a field. Go by the gate in the corner of the wood on your left and follow the track down through the wood, continue as it bends back sharp left and then bears right to meet a track along the flatter ground nearer the river. Go right along the track, leave the wood to pass through a small field and go towards the toilet block of the Scout Camp. Go left on the track here and continue through the remainder of the camp site and wood to cross a stile just after the track ends. (1500 metres)

Cross the field parallel to the right-hand wood and continue through the gate towards a footbridge at the confluence of the two infant Brock rivers. Do not cross the footbridge but turn right, pass the ruins of a former farmhouse, and go over the stile ahead. Continue above the river by the left-hand fence and go to cross a footbridge over a side clough stream. Beyond the bridge the path climbs gently through the wood to a stile over which you enter a field. In the field walk along by a line of old hedgerow trees with Parlick Pike directly ahead and cross the stile by the gate facing you. In the next field turn to follow the left-hand fence along to a stile by a gate in the left-hand corner of the field. Cross the stile

Bleasdale from the slopes of Parlick Pike

109

and go down the field, under the overhead power lines, by the right-hand boundary. Cross the stile in the right-hand corner and descend the steps to the road which, to your left, leads down to Bleasdale Post Office where refreshments can be obtained. (1500 metres)

To continue go past the post office, over the bridge and then turn right up the private Bleasdale Tower estate road. Follow the road to the school and on to the church. See Walk 12 if you wish to add Bleasdale Circle to your visit. Cross the cattle grid and then turn left to pass through two consecutive gates by Admarsh Barn. Follow the track down the field, pass the left-hand side of a small Scots pine copse, and continue down to a gate. Beyond the gate a track leads to the road which you follow to the right; cross the Brock by Brooks Farm, with its saddle (packhorse) bridge to your right, and continue upwards (ignoring any left turns) until you reach a right-hand road turning off at Brooks Barn Farm. (1700 metres)

Leave the road by the second of two gates on your left, go along a short track, through a gate, along by the left-hand fence below Bleasdale Tower, and through a further gate to enter a large field. Turn half left and go down and across this wet field to find a stone slab footbridge some 30 metres above the far field corner. Cross the slabs and the stile and go through the narrow wood which you leave by a further stile. In the field follow the right-hand fence around to a gate, through which you follow the track by the left-hand wall and

Hazelhurst Fell, Bleasdale

arrive, through a further gate, at Broadgate Farm. Go between the first buildings, turn right into the yard and then immediately left to a small gate that takes you past the front door of the farmhouse to a further gate and into the field beyond. (1300 metres)

Go up the field aiming for the far left-hand corner of the buildings at High Moor Farm. Go through the double gate at the corner of the building and pass through the yard of the farm, often used for stock and partially roofed over, to emerge on the farm access road that you follow to the road. Cross the road diagonally left and climb the stone stile to enter a field. (Those taking the short cut rejoin our walk here.) (600 metres)

Cross the field diagonally left to cross the fence by a ladder stile by a gate and then the next, very wet field towards the enclosed wood. You enter Huds Brook wood by a stone step stile to the right of the mid-point of the boundary wall, follow the path directly across wood and then re-enter the fields by a further stone step stile. Cross the field to a farm bridge over a small ditch and then aim 20 metres above the farm buildings to cross a stile with a tall marker post. Cross the middle of the next field by keeping parallel to the left-hand wall, go over a stile and then walk parallel to the right-hand fence to reach two adjacent stiles (only one useable). Over these climb the slight rise and then bear slightly right to cross another pair of stiles. Descend the next field besides the right-hand boundary to reach a road by a stile adjacent to the gate in the far right-hand corner. (1700 metres)

Cross the road and enter the field by the stile by the gate. Go half left and climb the hillock passing a bent oak tree, and then descend following the overhead power lines to reach the farm track, to the left of Foggs Farm, where it goes through a gateway. Cross the track directly and re-enter the field to again follow the overhead lines. Cross the stile to the right of the last power line pole and again follow the route of the power lines to find a stile which you cross in a fence corner. Go right in the field and follow the right-hand fence along to a gate and the road. (1200 metres)

Turn right along the road but soon leave it to the left to go along the access track of High House Farm. Follow the track and just after it bends left go through the gate on your right into a field. Go half left across the field aiming for a gate in the left-hand boundary towards the higher part of the field. Go through this gate and turn left to go to cross a further gate and stile over which you follow the right-hand fence to a further stile. Cross the stile and follow the left-hand boundary down to gate and then continue along an enclosed track. At the end go over the stile to your left and reach the road by the access drive to Clarkson's Farm. Turn right along the road, May Lane, and follow this for some 1300 metres, ignoring roads off to the left and then right, until you come to a right-hand bend by Brow Top. (2300 metres)

Go through the access gate to stone-built Brow Top, continue directly ahead through the gate by the barn and then go through the gate on the left to enter a field. Go half right to contour around the hilly field, and then follow the right-hand boundary down to reach the road by a stile to the immediate right of the white house. Turn left on the road and immediately over New Bridge turn right to retrace your original steps along the Brock to the A6 at Brock. (1800 metres)

A vaccary: is a small settlement where cattle where bred and land farmed on the king's behalf in the twelfth and thirteenth centuries. Names of these settlements are still in use today. In Upper Wyresdale there were twelve vaccaries and examples met on the walks include Tarnbrook, Catshaw, Emmett, Marshaw and Haythornthwaite.

Walk 14

Of Water and Abbots

Cockerham – Bay Horse – Glasson Dock – Cockerham

16.5 kilometres (10 miles) with a 13 kilometres (8 mile) shorter route

Start: Cockerham Centre (GR 465523). Alternatively Glasson Dock can be used for both routes. Bus passengers from Garstang and the south can alight at Bay Horse for the longer route.

Bus: Bay Horse is on the Lancaster – Garstang- Preston Service 40 & 41 route. Cockerham is served by the 88 Lancaster to Fleetwood and the 89 Lancaster to Poulton buses.

Car Parking: In Cockerham but not on a private car park.

Map: O.S. Pathfinder 659 Galgate and Dolphinholme

This walk has a variety of interests, especially the most scenic sections of the Lancaster Canal. Glasson Dock and Cockersand Abbey feature on both routes whilst the shorter route offers Thurnham Hall but misses much of the canal. This walk includes a section of the Lancashire Coastal Way.

From the centre of Cockerham walk south along the road from the Manor Inn and turn onto the footpath adjacent to house number 27. Go through the short

114

Walk 14: Of Water and Abbots

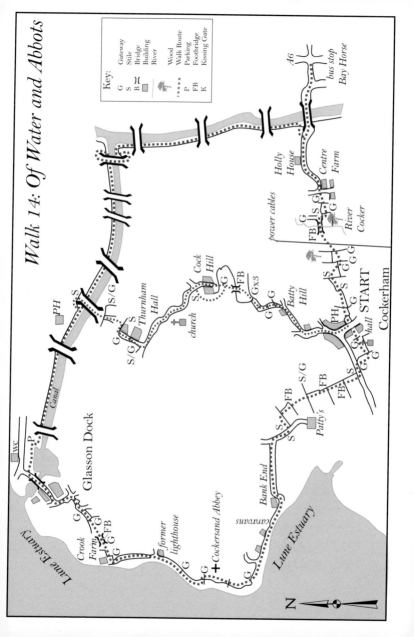

Key:
G   Gateway
S   Stile
B   Bridge
■   Building
~~~ River
🌲 Wood
···· Walk Route
P   Parking
FB Footbridge
K   Kissing Gate

Lune Estuary

Crook Farm

Glasson Dock

Canal

PH

Thurnham Hall

Cock Hill

church

Batty Hill

Holly House

Centre Farm

power cables

River Cocker

bus stop

Bay Horse

A6

former lighthouse

Cockersand Abbey

Bank End

caravans

Patty's

Lune Estuary

START

Cockerham

wc

N

garden, climb the stile and go through the gate by the top right of the barn. In the field follow the right-hand hedge up the hillock, a drumlin. (200 metres) From this rise there are extensive views of Wyresdale, Morecambe Bay, the Lakeland Fells and south towards Winter Hill.

Descend the hillock to cross a double stile where the hedge juts slightly into the field. Follow the hedge now on your left and cross a stile facing you just right of the field corner. Cross the next field diagonally to the gate in the far right-hand corner, by the corner of the wood, go through this gate, turn left and pass through a second gate. In the next field aim for the left-hand corner of the wood ahead, pass under the overhead power line and reach a footbridge to cross the River Cocker. (700 metres)

Follow up the right-hand edge of the wood, pass through a gateway and go over the stile on your right. Go up the field along the left-hand hedge and then through the gate facing you in the top corner. Cross the middle of the next field to pass through a gate at the rear of Centre Farm. (450 metres)

Go to follow the track ahead, with the farm buildings on your right. The enclosed track becomes metalled at Holly House Farm and then leads down to the canal. (1100 metres) Those using the bus along the A6 to Bay Horse/Potters Brook will join and leave the walk here for the short distance over the bridge to bus route.

The canal is now followed northwards, with the water on your right, until it comes to the high-arched bridge

Canal Junction, Galgate

over the Glasson branch. Cross the bridge and turn down left to follow the seven-locked branch some 4.4 kilometres to Glasson Dock. (6400 metres)

ⓘ *The canal stretch has adjacent woods, a rock cutting through the local sandstone, an attractive canal junction and with boating activity and wildlife along the way. The Lancaster Canal runs between the 50- and 100-foot contours and was built following a 1792 Act of Parliament. Its main users were industrial, agricultural and passenger traffic. Boats carried cargoes of coal north from Wigan and limestone south from Kendal. The bridges are a typical design of the builder Rennie, with a marked hump.*

On our way to Glasson Dock we pass Thurnham Mill, now

117

a hotel and bar. It was a water-powered corn mill driven by turbines and with a drying kiln on its north side. Water was taken from the canal, the race can be seen, but was originally extracted from the River Conder. In more recent times it became a cattle feed mill.

Glasson Dock is largely a product of the canal age and developed when the increasing size of ships and the silting of the Lune prevented ships using St George's Quay in Lancaster. The main dock was constructed by 1791 and was large enough to hold 25 large merchant ships. Some of the trade was with the West Indies. The branch canal was opened to the dock in 1826 and is notable for its tall wooden footbridges and the side weirs at the locks. The railway link with Lancaster took

Glasson Dock

away the canal trade but today the port is still commercially used and the village relies to some degree on tourism – especially at weekends.

The next section of the walk follows the well way-marked Lancashire Coastal Way. From the lock swing-bridge by the port follow the road up Tithebarn Hill to the viewpoint with an indicator and fine views across the estuary to Sunderland. Turn left at the top and then go right at the next crossroads near the farm with two prominent silo towers. Go down the enclosed lane, through some old gateposts and pass through a gate just beyond the caravan site entrance. (550 metres)

After passing through a second gate follow the track across the field, initially by the right-hand hedge, soon

Lune Estuary Lighthouse

119

largely derelict, but then bear left to pass over a gated bridge before you continue along the track by a left-hand hedge to the rear of Crook Farm. Go through the gate to the left of the farm buildings and then follow the farm access road to the left, along the Lune estuary, to a road junction by Lighthouse Cottage. (1750 metres) The area of the Lune and Cocker estuaries is a bird sanctuary and in winter with a flow tide can provide a spectacle of many thousands of waders.

Continue along the estuary-side track, which forms a sea defence wall, and via a series of kissing gates to eventually descend by a concrete ramp to the shoreline path at Bank House. (1750 metres)

🛈 *This path passes near to the remains of Cockersand Abbey with its Chapter House. This was a site established by the Premonstratensian Order in 1190 on where there had previously been a hospital. It was the abode of hermit Hugh Garth before it became a colony for lepers and the infirm. Dissolution came in 1539 when the house contained 22 priests, five aged and infirm men who were 'kept dayle of charitie', and 57 servants. The Chapter House (c.1230), with its vaulted roof held by clustered columns and leafy capitals, later became a burial vault for the Dalton family of Thurnham.*

🚶 Continue along the foreshore, pass the ruined buildings, the road end and then Cockerham Sands Caravan Park, and go on to reach a tarred road at Bank End Farm. Go ahead to follow the road besides the embankment,

Chapter House, Cockersand Abbey

turn right at the junction at the far end, and continue towards Pattys Farm and the parachute centre. Just before the final right-hand bend before the house go left up the first of two pairs of steps up the embankment. (2250 metres) Here we leave the Lancashire Coastal Way.

Climb the stile from the embankment and go by the right-hand fence to cross a further stile and footbridge. In the field behind the buildings of the parachute centre aim towards Cockerham Church to reach and cross a stile by a gate. In the next field follow the left-hand fence and dyke over two footbridges and, at the end of the third field, over a stile in the far left-hand field corner that gives access to the road. (800 metres)

Go left along the road and pass through the white

121

kissing gate to follow a path to your right that leads by the church. The church was rebuilt in 1910 by Paley and Austin and has some plague gravestones. Continue up the church access track to the village hall and the centre of the village, the start of the walk, lies to the left. (400 metres)

🚶 The shorter route often has some wet patches of path but it enables a view of Thurnham Church and Thurnham Hall. From Cockerham Village Centre go north towards Lancaster on the A588 and continue along the road after the pavement ends. Just after Batty Hill Cottage turn right to follow the track to Batty Hill Farm. Go through the yard and immediately after the front of the farmhouse take the left-hand branch of the track and go down the enclosed lane to pass through a gate. (800 metres)

The track follows the right-hand boundary, goes through a gate and continues to a gate in the far right-hand corner. Go through this gate and two further gates on this short enclosed track to re-enter the fields. Bear left in the field and cross it towards Cock Hill Farm (with the pylon directly inline behind the farm). Cross the boundary on your way by a footbridge and go to the yard of the farm. Pass through the buildings, with the house on your right, and emerge on the access track. (If the yard is wet bypass it by keeping to the left of all the buildings and rejoin the track by a stile.) (700 metres)

From Cock Hall Farm follow the access track and eventually pass the Roman Catholic church and then continue to find Thurnham Hall on your right. (1150 metres) The remote Thurnham Church with its Egyptian-style tomb is worth a few minutes' look if the door is open.

Thurham Hall was once the home of the Dalton family who were descended from Sir Thomas More and the house was originally a thirteenth-century pele tower and the centre of a 50,000-acre estate. In the sixteenth century it was altered to look like a small castle and it acquired a new front (the original wall is behind) and a chapel in the nineteenth century. In the wall is a 300-year-old vow, probably brought from Aldcliffe Hall: 'We are the Catholic virgins who scorn to change with the times' – the vow of two of eleven Dalton sisters during Protestant rule. The façade of the house is

Thurnham Hall

attractive but the extensive commercial activities of this time-share/country club detract from the countryside setting. The loss of an interesting eighteenth-century barn for the extensions is much to be regretted.

(🚶) Go right down the track that is parallel to the face of the house, pass over a stile by a gate and continue down to pass through the gate at the end of the track. Turn right and follow the fence a short distance to a stile but do not cross. Turn left and cross the field to an old enclosed lane that you follow to cross the stile by the gate at the end. Cross the next field to the white-railed bridge over the canal. Cross the bridge towards a stile but squeeze through the gap in the left-hand corner and descend, with care, to the towpath. Follow the canal, with the water on your left, to Thurnham Mill and Glasson Dock – this is also on the main route. (2750 metres)

Public Transport: most of the walks in this book are accessible from public transport. The service numbers are given with each walk. For up to date travel information you are strongly advised to telephone for times prior to travel. The relevant numbers are Stagecoach Ribble on 01772 886633 and Blackpool Transport 01253 477166. Information about the seasonally running Fleetwood to Knott End Ferry can be obtained from Fleetwood Tourist Information Centre 01253 773953.

Walk 15

When Canals and Railways Held Sway

Glasson Dock – Aldcliffe – Galgate – Glasson Dock

14 Kilometres (8.5 Miles) –with a slightly longer option
of 15 kilometres
Start: Glasson Dock (GR 445562)
Bus: The 88 Lancaster to Fleetwood, 89 Lancaster to
Poulton and the 225 Lanacster to Glasson Dock Services
take you to our start. Alternatively start in Lancaster.
Car Parking: This is readily available in Glasson Dock
*Maps: O.S. Pathfinder Sheet 659 Galgate and
Dolphinholme (with a small section on 648 Lancaster)*

This walk is mostly along the route of an old railway
track-bed and along the canal that are linked by a
quiet lane and field-paths. It is a walk for all seasons but
spring and autumn give life to the canalside woods. The
walk is much about transport through the ages and there
is often much wildlife to see, especially along the Lune
Estuary. The walk is mostly level and very suitable for
those who do not wish to concentrate too much on
finding their way. Part of this walk is used by the
Lancashire Coastal Way.

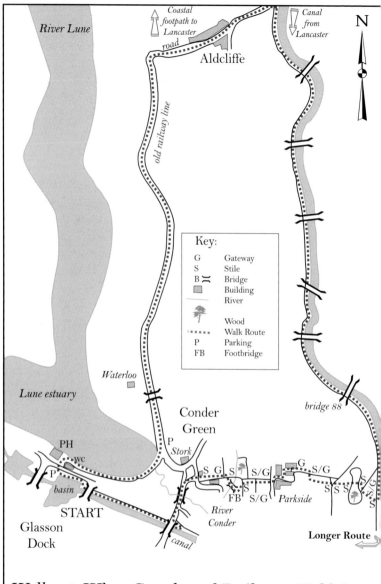

River Lune

Coastal
footpath to
Lancaster

road

Canal
from
Lancaster

N

Aldcliffe

old railway line

Key:

G	Gateway
S	Stile
B ⤵	Bridge
▢	Building
	River
🌲	Wood
▪▪▪	Walk Route
P	Parking
FB	Footbridge

Waterloo

Lune estuary

bridge 88

Conder
Green

PH

wc

P Stork

S G S   S/G   G S/G

S/G   S S S   S/G

P

basin

FB   S/G   Parkside   S   S

START

River
Conder

Glasson
Dock

canal

Longer Route

Walk 15: When Canals and Railways Held Sway

(🏃) From Glasson Dock go to the estuary side at the rear of the public toilets and, with the estuary on your left, walk along the route of the old railway. Continue through Conder Green car park and picnic site until you eventually reach the metalled road and information board just below Aldcliffe village. (5500 metres)

(ℹ) *The railway line from Lancaster to Glasson Dock was opened in 1890 and carried passenger services until 1930. It closed to freight in 1947 but the tracks were not raised until 1962. The only claim to fame of the line was that in 1917 King George V slept overnight on the royal train at Glasson. Trains to the dock were notorious for shaking a row of cottages near the port.*

Tales were told of railway firemen who used to kick out lumps of coal from their cabs when passing a fisherman's hut. Sometimes a salmon made the return journey. One engine driver was demoted after arriving at Lancaster only to discover that his carriages had been left at Glasson Dock station.

There were stations at Conder Green and one for Ashton Hall where you can still find the overgrown remains of the timber platform of Mr Starkie's halt, the then owner of the hall. Birdwatchers will need binoculars along this estuary-side path.

(🏃) Our way goes right up the metalled road through the village of Aldcliffe but see page 129 for an extension to and from Lancaster. At the top of the village go left at the road junction and follow the road down to meet the canal. Turn right, with the water on your left, to follow the towpath south all the way to the outskirts of Galgate which is marked, after bridge 88, by some houses and bungalows on the far bank of the canal. (5600 metres)

ⓘ *This well-wooded section of the canal is especially attractive in spring and autumn as the canal passes through a three-kilometre cutting to avoid the need for locks. In fact the main canal ran from Preston to Tewitfield for forty-eight kilometres before the first and only flight of locks to Kendal was reached. The bridges you pass under are fine half-elliptical examples of the work of the canal builder Rennie. One bridge you cross is where a stream is syphoned under the canal.*

⦿ Once opposite the first dwellings of Galgate cross a double stile in the hedge on your right. Go diagonally right across the field to pass over a stile by a gate in the boundary adjacent to the wood. Continue with the wood on your left and cross the stile on your left into the wood where the wood narrows. (250 metres)

Climb the path across the narrow Forerigg Wood and leave by the stile at the far side. In the field climb straight up the short, steep slope with a pylon seen ahead. Descend to cross the iron stile to the left of two trees in the boundary facing you. (250 metres)

Follow the right-hand hedge over a further stile, under the overhead power lines and up to cross through a stone gap-stile by a gate on your right. In this next field turn left and descend to the yard of Parkside Farm.

Pass through the yard via a gate adjacent to the right-hand silage clamp wall, turn left and then right to go to cross a stile by a gate in the boundary facing you across the track. (370 metres)

Follow the right-hand boundary, cross a stile by a gate and continue to cross a stile in the far right-hand corner of the second field adjacent to Crow Wood. Go ahead to cross the stiled stone slab footbridge and then immediately right to cross a stile on your right. In the next field turn left and follow the left-hand hedge up to pass through a gate and then down the next field to pass the rear of Webster's Farm and reach the road by a stile to the left of the small electricity sub-station building. (750 metres)

Go ahead on the road, turn left and follow the main road with care over the river bridge and then to the canal bridge. Go down left to the canal towpath and then turn right to go under the bridge and follow the towpath to Glasson Dock. (2000 metres)

❶ *For a slightly longer route, instead of turning off the canal (page 128) continue along the towpath until you reach the canal junction. Turn right and follow the Glasson branch of the canal all the way down to the start. This adds about 2.5 kilometres to the walk.*

A further alternative for this walk can be started at Lancaster. From Lancaster go to join the canal towpath to the south of the city centre and then continue as on pages 127–28. To return to Lancaster follow the route until the road end at *Aldcliffe* but go left over a stile at the end of the road. Follow the sign-posted Lancashire Coastal Way along the embankment path and then along to St George's Quay into Lancaster. This adds around 5 kilometres to the walk. O.S. map 648 Lancaster, would be useful for this extension.

Walk 16

The Shepherd's Church of Wyresdale

Abbeystead – Hawthornthwaite – Catshaw – The Shepherd's Church – Abbeystead

5.5 Kilometres (3.5 Miles)

Start: Abbeystead Hamlet by the School (GR 563543)

Bus: Service 146 or 147 Lancaster to Abbeystead.

Car Parking: Stoops Bridge – to the east of the school

Map: O.S. Leisure Sheet 41 Forest Of Bowland

---

superb, short walk around Upper Wyresdale amongst the fields and woods adjacent to Walk 2 of the book but rarely using the same paths. The two walks provide an excellent complement to Walk 1. This walk, suitable for most times of the year, visits Wyresdale church, better known as the Shepherd's Church, and provides views of the River Wyre and the Abbeystead Reservoir.

Abbeystead is named after the short-lived Cistercian abbey that was probably sited at the confluence of the Marshaw and Tarnbrook Wyres by monks from Furness Abbey. After a short period, during the twelfth century, the monks moved on to Ireland. Camden describes the scene here as 'solitary and dismal'. You may find solitude but the landscape is never dismal.

Walk 16: The Shepherd's Church of Wyresdale

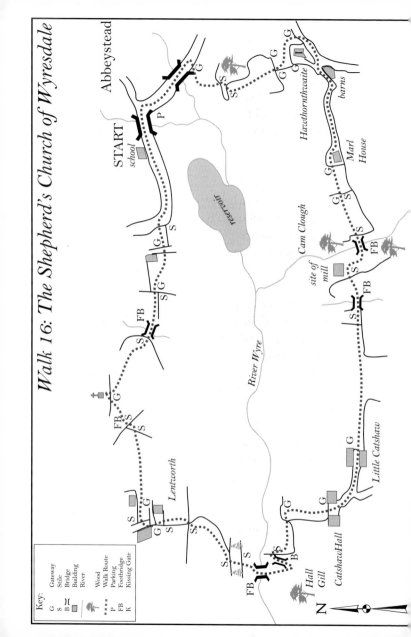

Abbeystead

START
school

reservoir

River Wyre

Lentworth

Hawthornthwaite

barns

Marl House

Cam Clough

site of mill

Little Catshaw

Catshaw Hall

Hall Gill

Key:
G   Gateway
S   Stile
B   Bridge
     Building
     River
     Wood
••• Walk Route
P   Parking
FB   Footbridge
K   Kissing Gate

N

From the centre of the hamlet, with the school to your left, go along the road, cross Stoops Bridge over the Tarnbrook Wyre and then turn right at the road junction where cars often park. Go down this road and cross the Marshaw Wyre. Just below the bridge the two upper Wyre streams join forces to carry their waters from the Bowland Fells down to the sea in Morecambe Bay. (250 metres)

Immediately over the bridge drop down right through an old gateway to follow the path through the woods. After two small footbridges go left on the right of way, ignoring a permissive path that carries straight on, and climb the wooded bluff up a series of steps. On top bear right to cross a stile and then follow the right-hand fence to cross the next stile. (250 metres)

Go left in the field and follow the left-hand fence along; go around the depression and then through the left-hand of two gates. In the next field also go through the left-hand of two gates and then along the right-hand boundary towards Hawthornthwaite Farm. The right of way passes to the immediate right of the farmhouse but arrows encourage the walker down to the left on the nearside of the house and then right through a gate up to the road. Go right on the road and, after the farm, right along a track to climb towards the modern barns. Go right over the cattlegrid at the nearside of these buildings and follow the track along to reach Marl House Farm. (1000 metres)

From this farm track are extensive views of the amphitheatre *of the upper Wyre catchment, and Abbeystead House, the shooting home of the Duke of Westminster, can also be seen in its woodland setting by the river.*

(✶) Continue along the track to the right of the farmhouse, pass through the gate facing you and cross the stile by the gate ahead of you. In the next field follow parallel to the left-hand fence and eventually go down to a stile and subsequent footbridge over the interesting beck in Cam Clough. (400 metres)

(ⓘ) *The rocks of the bed of Cam Clough show the wonderful carving action of the down-rushing stream. The smoothness, texture and shape are worth pausing to see. Climb the few steps ahead, then follow the embankment to the right and then, towards its end, it bends left and ends by some ruined buildings in the trees. The embankment was the former wall of a reservoir that served the buildings, the remains of an old cotton mill with waterpower. The mill burned down in the mid-nineteenth century. Some cottage walls also can be seen.*

(✶) Climb ahead up through the remains of the wood with the buildings to your right. Cross the stile in the fence ahead, cross the narrow field directly ahead to go down to cross a footbridge and then climb some stone steps and a stile. (300 metres)

In the next field follow the left-hand fence, a former lane, and then continue in the same direction along the farm track to arrive, through a gate, into the farmyard of Little Catshaw (1763). On your way a carved way-mark stone with a ram's head is passed. Bear right on leaving the yard and follow the road to the yard of Catshaw Hall Farm (1678). (850 metres)

🛈 *The hall was an ancient manorial residence and an older farm on this site, like Hawthornthwaite, was listed in 1324 as a vaccary (cattle farm). The building has charm and vernacular interest and still contains some ancient woodwork including a black oak staircase thought to be as old as the house.*

🚶 The gate facing you at the end of the yard leads you into a field that you descend straight down by the left-hand hedgerow to a gated depression above some trees. Go left through the gate, down an old track that heads to the river. Short of the river go left over a stile in the fence, cross the footbridge over Hall Gill and then follow the path along and right to go down to cross the metal-sided Long Bridge over the River Wyre. (600 metres)

🛈 *Whilst by the Wyre look for the white bib of the passing dipper or watch it, perched bobbing on a river-side boulder. The yellow wagtail or the flashing blue iridescence of the kingfisher may be spotted.*

🚶 From the footbridge cross the narrow field to climb a stile, climb the steps through the wood and then leave

Waymark below Abbeystead Church

by the stile at the top. In the field cross the track and follow near the right-hand fence as it climbs up the field. Cross the stile in the top right-hand field corner and arrive at a seat. Follow the left-hand fence to a stile at the rear of Lentworth House Farm.

After passing through the next two gates emerge on the track by the farmhouse. The farmhouse and subsequent stone waymarks all display interesting artistic features. (500 metres)

Opposite the end of the house cross the first of two stiles on your right, follow the left-hand wall, noting the weather vane. After the wall bends away left continue in the same direction (heading for the grey barns ahead) until the field dips down via a carved stone, where you cross two consecutive stiles and a footbridge. Climb the field to enter Wyresdale churchyard. (550 metres)

Christ Church is the Shepherd's Church. It sits high above the Wyre with its gargoyle waterspouts leaning out from the squat tower of local stone. The church site dates back to at least the fourteenth century. The church was rebuilt in 1733, but when the estate passed to the Sefton family, it was extended.

And suddenly there was with the Angel a multitude of the heavenly host, praising God, and saying, Glory to God in the highest, and on earth peace, good will toward men

The pulpit dates from 1684. The church is usually locked but the vicarage lies adjacent. Inside the church porch you can see wooden bars with iron hooks used by the shepherds to hang their crooks and lanterns. The windows date from the turn of the century and represent biblical pastoral scenes but set in the local landscape. All feature sheep. On display is a 'Geneva' bible printed in 1599, being so named after the place where the bible was translated into English during times of persecution under Mary Tudor in this country. It is also called the 'breeches bible'. This is due to the modesty of the translators, as we read in Genesis 3 verse 7, that Adam and Eve made themselves breeches.

Just above the church and vicarage is the Sunday School housed above the public stable. The original 1733 vicarage lies further to the north.

⊛ Return to the gate by which you entered the churchyard and go half left down the field again, aiming for the grey-roofed farm buildings. In the bottom far corner of the field cross the stile and then a footbridge. Climb up from the stream and go left by the old hedge line to a gate and stile, again aiming for the grey barns. Go over the stile and aim half right to reach the right-hand side of the lowest building. Cross the concrete road beyond the building and go through the gate in the wall opposite. Cross this last field to a stile in the far right-hand corner and then descend right along the road to Abbeystead and your start. (750 metres)

Walk 17

Exploring Bleasdale from Beacon Fell

Exploring Bleasdale – from Beacon Fell
13.1 Kilometres (8 Miles)
Start: Visitor Centre on Beacon Fell (GR 565427)
Bus: The nearest stop is Whitechapel on the 20 Garstang
to Longridge and Goosnargh Thursday only service
Car Parking: In the vicinity of the Beacon Fell Country
Park Visitor Centre
Map: O.S. Leisure Sheet 41, Forest of Bowland

This walk starts and finishes near its highest point.
It affords excellent views of the Bowland fells,
Pendle, the Darwen Moors and Winter Hill. On a good
day the views of the Lakeland Hills and the Isle of Man
can be superb. The walk around Bleasdale provides good
views of this upland parish and an opportunity to visit
the site of the Bleasdale Circle (see Walk 12 for details).
A possible fellwalking extension is suggested for those
suitably equipped.

Take the slanting path up from the visitor centre and
then turn left to walk the surfaced path to the summit
of the fell. The summit 'trig point' contains a viewpoint

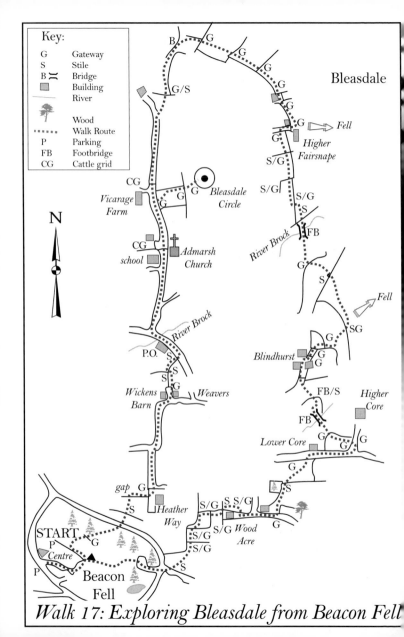

Key:

G — Gateway
S — Stile
B ≍ — Bridge
▢ — Building
— River
🌲 — Wood
······· — Walk Route
P — Parking
FB — Footbridge
CG — Cattle grid

N

Bleasdale

B
G
G
G
G
G
G/S
Fell
Higher
Fairsnape
S/G
S/G
S/G
S
S
River Brock
FB
G
S
Fell
SG
G
G
Blindhurst
G
FB/S
Higher
Core
FB
Lower Core
G
G
G
G

CG
Vicarage
Farm
G
G
Bleasdale
Circle
CG
school
Admarsh
Church
River Brock
P.O.
S
S
S
G
Wickens
Barn
Weavers

gap
G
S
Heather
Way
S/G
S
S/G
S/G
S
S/G
S/G
Wood
Acre
G
G
S
S

START
P
G
Centre
P
Beacon
Fell
S

Walk 17: Exploring Bleasdale from Beacon Fell

indicator. Turn right at the summit and follow the surfaced ridge path down to eventually emerge at the Quarry Car Park on the eastern side of the fell. Go down through the car park and along the access road until you meet the road that circles the fell. (1300 metres)

Go left on the road and immediately turn right down the side road. Follow the short left-hand wall for 20 metres and then climb the stile where the wall joins a fence. Go half-right down the field, in the direction of Parlick Pike, to meet a fence corner with a rough, sunken track beyond. Go left down the track, often very wet, as it continues by the left-hand fence. This is followed over two stiles by gates. There is a stile and gate on your left, which you do not cross, but continue along the track as it bends to the right. After the bend, go left over a further stile by a gate and walk down the field by the left-hand boundary towards a further stile by a gate – but do not cross them. (1100 metres)

Instead turn right and follow the fence formerly facing you, and now on your left, pass over the stile by the gate facing you as you continue to the rear of the buildings at Wood Acre. In the next field cross the stile on your left in the far left-hand corner of the field. Turn right along the boundary to pass the buildings and then climb the stile by the gate on your right. Go left down the access track to meet the road. Go straight ahead at this junction to pass Watery Gate Farm on your left. (500 metres)

Continue just past Watery Gate and go through the

gate on your left just prior to the start of the roadside wood. Go forward along the wood edge and then go to follow the left-hand fence along the field. Cross the stile in the fence facing you near the field corner and then go half right in the next field to reach the road by a gate opposite the barn of Lower Core Farm that comes into view when crossing the last field. Turn right and go up the road until you reach the gated access track to Lower Core Farm on your left. (1200 metres)

Go up the access track but soon leave it through the first gate on your left. Follow along by the right-hand wall and pass through the gate in the fenced section in the field corner. Cross the next field aiming for Blindhurst Farm ahead and, in a depression at the far side of the field, cross the footbridge. Turn right in the next field and follow the right-hand boundary around until you see a stile in a small section of stone wall. Cross the stile and the subsequent footbridge and then cross the field to the access track and follow it up to the yard of Blindhurst Farm. (950 metres)

ⓘ *Blindhurst Farm has a 1731 datestone and its architectural style, with cross windows and three-lighted mullion and transomed windows, reflects the age of its construction. There is another farmhouse to the left – it is said that two brothers fought over the same land and when one brother built a house, the other responded likewise.*

⊛ Go to the right of the whitewashed farmhouse and follow the track through two gates to emerge into a small field. Turn right and go up the field to pass through a further gate. Go towards the wall in the next field but then branch left along the 'concessionary' footpath that climbs a distinct track steeply up to cross the stile by a gate. [For those with more energy this concessionary path can be continued upwards to the col to the north of Parlick. The ridge leads north to the Paddy's Pole top of Fairsnape Fell from where a further path leads down to Higher Fairsnape Farm and re-connects with our route.] Our way goes to the left where the track leads down to a fence at a track junction. Cross the stile in the fence facing you and then go down right to a lower track that leads right over a small stream. (500 metres)

Just over the stream leave this track and go along the left-hand fence and through the first gate. Aim just right of the farm ahead towards a small clump of trees. Amidst this clump a footbridge takes you over the infant River Brock and then cross a stile. Follow the left-hand fence along until you reach a stile and a gate. Cross the stile, turn right and follow the fence again, now on your right. Cross the stile by the gate in the right-hand field corner and continue along a track by the right-hand fence, cross over a further stile and gate and then along to pass through a gate and reach the access road to Higher Fairsnape Farm. Turn right towards the farm, pass through the gate, and continue to pass the stone barn on your left. (1200 metres)

ⓘ *Higher Fairsnape is the possible site of a vaccary and two seventeenth-century houses can be seen. The date-stone above the main house is very elaborate and is dated 1637 with the initials of the Parkinson family, the owners at that time.*

ⓧ Pass the left-hand barn and turn left along the track, go through the gate facing you and then aim to pass through the gate to the immediate right of the barn. Continue along the distinct track by the left-hand fence and continue in the same direction after a further gate. A gate, directly ahead, leads you into a third field but the track is less firm and you follow it down parallel to the left-hand wall. Leave this field by the gate facing you and then go down by the right-hand boundary to a track junction. (850 metres)

Go left down the track a 'concessionary' path over the stream and then follow the left-hand fence to a gate and stile. Over the stile go ahead to pick up the estate road. Follow this road up to pass the cattle grid at Vicarage Farm (with access to Bleasdale Circle) and then along and down past the church, school and village hall and continue over the next cattle grid and down to the country road. Go left to reach Bleasdale Post Office and café. (2500 metres) Information about the Bleasdale Circle and the church are to be found in walk 12.

Continue past the post office and climb up the road until a flight of steps on your right leads you up to a stile and then into a field. Follow the left-hand boundary and cross the stile by the gate on your left in the corner of

Bleasdale from Parlick Pike

the field. Turn right and follow the fence, now on your right, to a gate at the rear of the buildings of Wickens Barn Farm. Go through the gated yard to the road that you follow to the right. Just after a right-hand bend turn left down an access road signed Broadhead. When the track forks go directly ahead through the gate and along the drive of Heatherway. When you are opposite the house with its ugly, large windows turn right through a gate. (1500 metres)

Follow the left-hand fence but after 100 metres go left, at a path junction by a former gateway in the fence, and strike up the field to a stile below the trees of Beacon Fell. Cross the stile, go ahead to the road that circles the fell and cross it diagonally right to a forest track and barrier. Go up this track beyond the barrier and leave the forest area through a small gate by the large gate where the surfaced track ends. Go directly ahead over a track and climb the rougher track over open fell land towards the trees ahead. When the trees are reached go left back to the top of Beacon Fell and, after enjoying the view, turn right to descend back to the information centre. (1500 metres)

Walk 18

The Last of the Fylde Mosses

Winmarleigh – Bone Hill – Winmarleigh

11.7 Kilometres (7 miles)
Start: Winmarleigh Church (GR 471480)
Bus: School Day only 567 and 581 Hambleton and Knott
End to Lancaster
Car Parking: Politely near Church
Map: O.S. Pathfinder Sheet 668, Garstang

This walk is virtually flat with the exception of the sporadic farmsteads being sited atop minor undulations in this former mossland landscape. The walk crosses the remnant of Winmarleigh Moss, a Site of Special Scientific Interest, that shows us what much of the land between the current A6 and the coast must have looked like a few thousand years ago. The farm of Bone Hill, passed on the walk, has a dark history. Despite the low-lying position of the land it can provide a dry walk and, in season, there are some notable displays of snowdrops.

From Winmarleigh Church go along the road towards the school, turn left down School Lane and, on the second right-hand bend in the road, turn left to go down

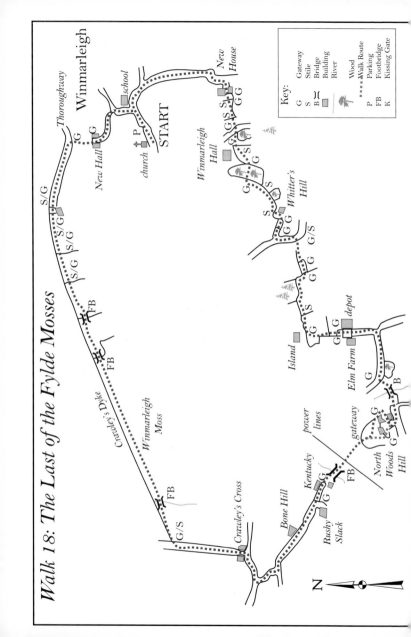

Walk 18: The Last of the Fylde Mosses

Winmarleigh

Thoroughfway

New Hall

school

church

P

START

New House

Winmarleigh Hall

Whitter's Hill

Island

Elm Farm

depot

power lines

gateway

North Woods Hill

Kentucky

Bone Hill

Rushy Slack

Crawley's Cross

Crawley's Dyke

Winmarleigh Moss

FB

G/S

G/S

S/G

S/G

S/G

S/G

FB

FB

G

G

S

S

S

S

G

G

G/S

G

G

G

S

G

G

G

G

B

G

G

G

G

G

S

FB

N

Key:

G	Gateway
S	Stile
B	Bridge
▪	Building
🌲	River
▪▪▪	Walk Route
🌲	Wood
P	Parking
FB	Footbridge
K	Kissing Gate

the access road to New Hall Farm. Go through the clean, cobbled farmyard to pass the farmhouse on your left and then go into a field by using the gate facing you. Follow the field down to pass through the obvious gate in the boundary across your way. (1400 metres)

Go left on the track – called Thorough Way – and follow it all the way to the gas pipeline installation. The name of the track hints at an ancient route but its possible origins lie in the removal of peat from the mosses for use as litter for poultry houses in the late nineteenth century, when two extraction companies were active. Cross the stile to the immediate right of the gate and follow between the right-hand dyke and the fenced site to enter the fields by a further stile by a gate. In the first field follow along the right-hand dyke to cross the stile by the gate in the far right-hand corner. Continue along the dyke in the next two fields, also by way of a stile and gate, and this leads to a footbridge in the far right-hand field corner. Use this to cross the main dyke coming from the left and then continue along the line of the right-hand dyke, as it becomes narrower, to cross a further footbridge in the far right-hand corner of the field. (2000 metres)

❶ *The dyke we have been following is named Crawley's Dyke and later we come to Crawley's Cross Farm where nearby lies Crawley's Cross, a boundary marker.*

❀ The path continues, in the same direction, as close along the side of the right-hand dyke across Winmarleigh Moss as the ground conditions allow.

ⓘ *The path slightly wanders between tufty grasses and birch trees that are colonising the drying mossland. The peat soils are very evident. Some remains of the heather and bog myrtle can be seen. In summer watch out for butterflies.*

⚲ Eventually the moss on the right-hand of the dyke gives way to fields, the moss path goes through more open ground and then a footbridge enables you to leave the mossland.

In the field continue to follow the right-hand dyke and fence to leave by a stile and gate in the far right-hand field corner. (1800 metres)

Turn left on the track and then join the road by Crawley's Cross Farm. Turn right along the road but take the first left-hand turn into Bone Hill Lane. Go along this cul de sac, go over the bridge, turn left at the junction and continue by way of Bone Hill until the track bends sharply right to Rushy Slack Farm. Our way continues straight ahead down the access track that leads to Kentucky Farm. Go through the yard, pass the front of the house, and leave by the gate at the far end. (1700 metres)

ⓘ *Bone Hill Farm has a dark history for during the eighteenth and nineteenth centuries there lived a family whose notoriety, claims one historian, 'rivalled the Doones of Exmoor'. Among several infamous pursuits, it is claimed, the family ran a 'baby farm'. It was here that the embarrassment of the rich and noble families — the unwanted offspring of daughters and mistresses — were disposed of, or, if the right fee was paid, reared to maturity. The head of the Bone Hill family, recognised by a white feather in his hat, would meet his clients in Garstang. Perhaps the path we now use was the way the mothers walked across the mosses to Bone Hill. The farm was also the site of a cock fighting main. A prehistoric bog burial was found in the vicinity of Bone Hill.*

🚶 Go forward in the field but bear right to find a footbridge across the dyke behind the water-pumping site. In the next field (a large arable field but the crops should not obscure the path) aim towards the rear of North Wood's Hill Farm and pass under the overhead power cables almost midway between two pylons. The old hedge line below the farm is reached. Go through the gateway to enter this enclosed area. The right of way heads across towards the right-hand side of the farm, enters the farmyard by a gate and goes left past the front of the house. However the track from the gateway follows the left-hand hedge line and then branches right into the gated farmyard and comes out towards the farmhouse. From here go down the short farm access road to the road, New Lane. (1100 metres)

Go left down the road and where it bends right to become Woods Lane leave the road by going directly ahead by the right-hand hedge to cross a footbridge adjacent to a farm-bridge and gate. Cross the next field diagonally left to pass through a gate on the immediate left of the small wood with a few notable Scots pine trees. Go right on the busy road, Black Lane, but when it bends sharp right cross it carefully and go left down Station Lane. This is named after the former Nateby Station and the remains of the station platform can just be seen in the garden of the bungalow. Follow the road along to Elm Farm, sometimes with a barrier across the road, as this is now a major haulage depot. Go along to pass through the next barrier to the left of the large buildings. (1000 metres)

Before the end of the buildings go to the right of a hedge whose abrupt end faces you and follow it along (the hedge on your left) to pass through a gate. Continue up the field by the left-hand hedge, go through the gate and continue by the left-hand hedge, aiming directly for Island Farm, but when the boundary bends away to the left continue towards the gate directly below the farm. Do not pass through this gate but turn right and follow the boundary on your left until it goes down to a field corner in a hollow. Cross the stile facing you and continue by the left-hand boundary and up by the left-hand wood. Go down to the far left-hand field corner, turn to your right and follow this boundary to pass through the second gate on your left some 50 metres from the field corner. (800 metres)

Through this gate go along the left-hand dyke side, pass through a further gate and continue with the dyke

Winmarleigh sunset

on your left until you can leave the field by the stile by the gate. Go left along the road but soon turn right, over a brick-lined arched bridge, and follow the gated access track that leads up to Whitters Hill, a private house. On entering the grounds of the house turn left and go between the boundary and the front of the house to reach a stile over a high gate facing you. In the field go right and follow the right-hand boundary to pass a wood, a field boundary with a stile and then alongside a long wood. To the left is the unsightly field, tipped with concrete pipes etc., of Gift Hall. Look for a small swing gate in the wood boundary, pass through the narrow wood and leave by the swing gate at the far side. In the field bear left to walk parallel to the left-hand boundary as it passes the front of Winmarleigh Hall, and go to cross an iron ladder stile to the left of the field gate. Continue by the side of the right-hand wood and leave the field by a small gate in the far right-hand corner. (1200 metres)

❶ *Paley designed Winmarleigh Hall in 1871 for the Patten Family from Warrington. The owner became the first, and the last, Lord Winmarleigh, for ill luck dogged the family. The house was four storeys, of red brick with a cloister-like loggia. Partial rebuilding occurred after a fire in 1927.*

🚶 Cross the road directly through a further small gate and walk ahead in the field, with Nicky Nook in the distance and the farm roof also ahead, to cross a further iron stile. Follow the right-hand fence down to cross a stile and two gates to enter the yard of New House Farm. Go through the yard to reach the road by way of the front of the farmhouse. Turn left along the road and keep left at the junction to return to your start. (1500 metres)